The Council Estate Kid

The Chronicles of Dodger

The Council Estate Kid

Stephen J. English

First published in 2021

Copyright © 2021 by S.J.English

Conditions of sale

This book is sold subject to the condition that it shall not, by way of trade or otherwise, be lent, re-sold, hired out or otherwise circulated without the publisher's prior consent in any form of binding or cover other than that in which it is published and without a similar condition including this condition being imposed on the subsequent purchaser.

Dedication

This book is dedicated to my Mum Eileen Georgina English.

Acknowledgements

The Chronicles of Dodger Fifty five years in the making. The Council Estate Kid twenty one years in creation!

I am self-taught and this has been arduous, challenging and a stern examination of the inner will. Firstly my gratitude to my parents John and Eileen English. Sadly my Mum has passed away but she will always be my Goddess in the Elysian fields. Your toughness of yesteryear is my strength 'in the presence'. The love that my Dad has given me remains beyond words. I have hurt my parents by my own foolishness but they always love me unconditionally because I am their son. My Sister Julie Robinson Williams who again there are not many words to explain the love we have for each other. My niece and nephews. Robert, Kieran, Morgan and Harrison. who just love Uncle Dodge for being Uncle Dodge. My lifelong friend Stephen Morgan, both kids from the Surrey Lane Estate, our friendship has been fifty years; how lucky are we! Martin 'the Music Man' Richards who supported me at a low point of my life. The Great George Stanley Ennor who taught me hard smart graft leads to success. His son, my life long friend Deano, for being a proper good mate. Khalid Mair who encouraged me to write and not deny to the reader my perspective on life. Miss Celia Guppy who not only supported me in the writing arena but also saw a story in my pictures, which I did not see myself. Then we get to a kindred spirit. My captain from my youth footballing days Richard Mckenzie. Our paths parted but somehow we are both together working as a team again. Richard and I go back forty-six years and he has definitely been the yang to my yin. He is my writer & artist agent, manager, music producer and editor (and introduced me to the use of the predicate and syntax, which is very helpful for storytelling!). Thank you my friend for helping me navigate the good ship Dodger.

I have to say a big thanks to the HarperCollins family for their twin sons 'Dictionary' and 'Thesaurus'; these have been by my side constantly on the pilgrimage in becoming a writer. The books of Carl Jung helped me understand how to free the unconscious from the negative past and release the inner child of the active imagination and to encourage it to flow without limitations. Mr William Shakespeare for showing me the frailties of the human condition. Mr William Blake for allowing me to believe I can write meaningful prose as an emotive art that connects with others on a deeper level. Up until the 13th of February 2021 I didn't even know I could draw. Lastly because I can whittle on, I reflect back over many years working as a lorry driver and delivering building supplies. I've done my hard graft including as a lorry driver in the winter with hands frozen unloading 2000 second hand yellow building bricks.

Every day I am blessed. To write and draw is an absolute joy. But, within my heart will always reside 'The Council Estate Kid'.

Contents

The Council Estate Kid!	10
In The Beginning there was Dodger	13
The Renaissance Kid	21
The Estate on the Battersea Bridge Road	30
Waiting for Dodgot	42
I am the Goalkeeping Paradox	46
The Village Brings Up the Child	53
Playing Out and Playschemes – All is One!	60
Artistic Football – A Man with a Plan	74
The Collective Heart of the People	80
A Pupil of Indifference or a Unique Thinker?	88
An Ode to our Peculiar Colloquialisms	93
Escape from the City	99
Death is not the Opposite of Life	111
Chosen Subjects?	118
Notable Brief Encounters	124
A Women for all Seasons and Reasons	131
Free the Hastings Three!	142
The Past and The Present - What were the Lessons?	152
Battersea	160

Introduction

The Council Estate Kid!

The oldest form of learning is from storytelling and listening, and in retrospect, this is a performance art. These are the stories and observations of the adventurous life of 'Dodger' (yes that's me!). They also include family members, friends, places and events that shaped me from an early age.

I have personally experienced drug addiction (amphetamines, MDMA, Cannabis), nervous breakdown and psychosis. I was sectioned for seven weeks in psychiatric hospital, two years in my bedroom with clinical depression, panic attacks, anxiety, and agoraphobia and went from 16 stone down to 10 stone and finally homelessness. For a period of seven challenging years Dodger found himself looking after mum with dementia. She passed away at 2.08pm on the 15th May 2020. When mum was first diagnosed her words were, '*I may have memory problems but I am not blooding stupid, this cruel illness is just another stage of life*'. I was the main carer for my Mum, my guiding light, she passed peacefully at home, and I was the only one with her when she took her last breath. She waited for my Sister to pop home, my Dad to go out of the room, my Mum knew her baby boy could deal with the emotional and mental responsibility of sharing her last moments on the material plain. I stared death in the face and it did not scare me, death makes life more important, it was the most challenging and heart breaking yet most fulfilling and rewarding experience of my life. My Mum in her final weeks told me, *'Butch (her affectionate name for me), I'm tired'*. I said, *'then go mum'*. She replied, *'you have been and always will be my baby boy, you have been a good son, although you were a nuisance at times. I love you (which she had never told me before) please take care of my John (her husband, my Dad).'*

This was my duty then and I carried out her wish and, hopefully, anyone reading this story will understand that compassion, forgiveness, gratitude, kindness, non-judgement, peace of mind and unconditional love does get you through the most traumatic life events; oh and did I say that with a sprinkling of humour. Try to love with your heart and let your brain follow, endeavour not to base your inner happiness on all the external material objects; it's not a truth! Rather, embrace the simple 'free' things because they form the most important essence of our being. Try to love every day, everyone suffers because that is part of our existence. Life is a dance not a destination so give help, guidance and support to others who need and do this without expectation. Be courageous if needs be and say 'no' to something or someone and consider an explanation is not always needed. Never ever take anything for granted in life. Always remember we are not here for a long time, we are here for a good time! Just a little thought for contemplation, when I go and visit both sets of grandparents at the cemetery and browse all the departed souls, not one headstone quotes that the person lying therein was a good worker!

Know thyself and Love thyself. Are you sitting comfortably? Let the story commence.

Luv Dodger xx

Chapter One

In The Beginning there was Dodger

My name is Stephen John English (Dodger to my family and friends), writer, storyteller and lover of wisdom. I was born on the 26th of April 1966 at 27 Crampton House, Patmore Estate which was a tough inner city affair. This was the same day that William Shakespeare was baptised, though a mere 400 hundred years later. Dodger was delivered in my parents' bedroom, to John Frederick English and Eileen Georgina English (nee James). Alas, my father was not at this momentous occasion because he was at Stamford Bridge watching Chelsea play Aston Villa. If my Mum was not giving birth to me, she would have definitely been at the Bridge as well.

I was born into a working class family, but that should never define you as a person, as George Orwell (Eric Blair) quoted in the road to Wigan Pier, *'you get more intelligence and wisdom in a working class pub on a Saturday night than you would get with all the intellectual elite'.* I am not the only sibling as I already had an older sister Julie, at 6 years older, but wanted a little sister and was not happy. No wonder why, at a very tender age she did so happen to drop me on my head, on purpose or not, and let me jump off a wall and break my arm and collarbone whilst again in her care. From then, and still presently, she referred to me as her baby brother; despite me being six foot three. We will be forever protective of each other. The black and white photos we have in the family albums are either my sister eating or me with a persona of a miserable little git! It took Dodger quite some time to speak, and I worked out later in life this was due to my sister who does not ever stop, just like Mrs. Honeyman in the old *'Watch with Mother'* children's series of the 1960 and 1970 called *'Camberwick Green'*. There were many pictures of me, at my elder cousin's wedding, not smiling, non-conformist pageboy, peach satin blouse, black satin trousers, looking like the seventh member of the Osmonds and not too happy about the situation. Why they dressed me up like that as a child, heaven knows, I suppose a paradigm was fixed back then and unconsciously I have never had the burning desire to get hitched. Even my nanny Ivy English told me when I was about seven years old *'don't get married boy, have the freedom to do what you want, when you want'!* I have been engaged several times. Later on my path, finding me in my middle age and still under the same roof as my folks, an enormous responsibility dawned and allowed me to step up to the big duty, and unbelievable challenge, of taking care of my irreplaceable Mother.

In these chronicles all the positive individuals who have enriched and taught me ethical, principled and valuable life lessons without really knowing their importance, (what I call wisdom guides) will be named because they mean so much to me. Those others, who caused the most negativity and pain, will remain anonymous. Why? As one of my life mantra goes, if you keep having the same negative experience, same situations, same people, you haven't learnt the life lesson. This is called an unconscious paradigm that has not been changed so you are thinking in the past. This is how depression starts by not living in the presence (yes I do mean 'presence'). A little interesting fact, what I like to call my miscellaneous filing system, is that we have roughly sixty five thousand thoughts a day and ninety five percent are repeated daily. We are the greatest computer ever made!

One of my earliest memories is riding my bike over Battersea Park at an area known locally as the *'monkey hills'* which runs parallel with Chelsea Bridge Road adjacent to the running track. Knocking myself spark out coming down about a seven in one gradient, fearlessly stupid I will call it, being carried home by Dad and out for the count. I was met by a concerned woman on Battersea Dogs Home bridge asking my dad if I was in a coma. I woke up for a second, told the women to piss off and then fell back into an unconscious state. Finally I was awoken in the bath at home surrounded by my family members and definitely stating I was 'Hank Marvin' (starving).

Being born to a very big circle of extended family, The English's, Cook's and James's there were always great grandparents, great uncles, and aunts still alive. My oldest Great Grandfather was Michael Sinjin Cook, Mike for short, a true Battersea character who had experienced two world wars and could still take care of himself into his nineties. This was demonstrated when he gave a young mugger a good hiding. He could always earn a pound note but was not free spending with money. He and my great grandmother Elizabeth Cook had 11 children. All were born at Latchmere Grove and my Mum's mum 'Nanny James' was one of them. All of the properties were demolished due to slum clearance of the 1950's and 1960's. This led to the numerous council estates in Battersea. Though no longer, and since my childhood been swallowed up by Wandsworth, Battersea was its own borough. I don't come from Wandsworth, I am a Battersea boy. I am not a cockney. I come from south London, which has a different structure to its dialect than the rest of London. I can tell east London from south London just by listening.

Nursery witnessed my first outbreak of non-compliance but it did not last long though the shackles of conformity helped make me a rebel. Then followed the experience of state education at Sir James Barrie School where from day one I was a nuisance. Many a time my sister had to come from her class because I was playing up. I believe that's where my maverickship started; battling against the norm and being forced into a way of learning and thinking only fit for the world of low paid and menial employment. More recently, I have reflected on how this helps develop the fundamental attributes and life skills needed for a fulfilling life.

At school one of our regular pursuits was country dancing. Country dancing what was that about? Skipping around to Scottish music in my underpants and vest! What prompted this laugh of a lesson? Firstly, we were not in Scotland, no way a judgment of Scottish dancing, but what social significance did that have to my upbringing? Totally baffled and embarrassed beyond belief both boys and girls in underwear dancing and prancing like a druid summer solstice for under-fives. After some research it turns out the reason involves a minister of education thinking it would have a positive impact on children's lives! Yes, it would be if I had dreams to be a Morris dancer. Now when I was in a field in 1989, raving with ten thousand other souls my mind did not reflect back and think *'oh flip I am so glad I did country dancing'*! Musical movement another wasted educational pursuit. It's funny what you remember. The teacher would say '*engage your inner expression of your true being*'! Now that's a bit deep in philosophical terms for a four year old to understand whose highlight of the day was 'Trumpton' and 'Mary, Mungo and Midge'. And this still remains the fundamental flaw in education. A minister as a politician had never lived or would ever likely understand the mindset of ordinary working class people. This is true to this day and that is why I have never voted. My only joy and remembrance of this period of schooling were the nativity plays. This is where my acting went from a shepherd to king. Then there was the harvest festival playing a pig and these remained my highlight of two years at Sir James Barrie.

The year was 1971, my Mum's dad 'Grandfather' George James had just died after working hard all his life. In World War Two he was in the bomb disposal division and fighting in Arnhem. He returned to the UK to defend a coal mine in Wales but instead of following orders he ended up giving it free to all the locals! He retired from hard labour as a bricklayer and six months later dropped dead from a heart attack. He never got any time to enjoy any sort of retirement. This experience has shaped me and so I say work hard when young because you have the stamina but as you get older work smart. We had to move from the Patmore Estate due to my sister and I sharing a bedroom. We were moving to the brand new council estate The

Surrey Lane which was at the other end of Battersea next to Battersea Bridge Road. A massive estate still not fully finished made up of maisonettes and tower blocks. We moved into 18 Sancroft Court, which was named after William Sancroft (1617-1693) former Archbishop of Canterbury. All estate block names had a reference to so called 'righteous' religious figures; the individuals with influence and money and little common sense!

In those days we could not afford a removal company for our move, so a Mk1 Ford Luton transit was hired and all of us mucked in and especially my cousin Georgie Williams. As a man he was of a high natural intelligence such that the broadsheet newspaper crosswords were a doddle. He enjoyed a beer, was family oriented, and played an important part in my life. A man loved by everyone, he drank in the Balham Park Hotel and was the only white man in there. His best friend was called Roderick Broderick, a Jamaican man who just loved George to bits; connection made from the heart not from the judgmental mind. As we were just finishing the last load of stuff to our new home everyone was gasping for a cup of tea. Unbeknown to all of us when asked by my Mum about the whereabouts of the kettle Georgie replied '*I dropped it out of the back of the Luton and a 49 bus ran right over it and squashed it… Sorry Aunty*'. But we had our cup of tea, boiling a saucepan of water, proper tea leaves and all refreshed. The end of the world could be upon us but as long as the British have a cup of char everything will be fine.

I had the smaller room of the three bedroom maisonette and my sister the larger because she had to have 'OK' our rocking horse. My dad had won it in The Sun newspaper where an original name had to be given to an imaginary racehorse. Dad gave the name 'OK', after the cockney rhyming slang for horse, rocking horse 'sauce' ('OK' being a brand of sauce). And did so he only went and won it! We could have chosen a real life pony. Yes that would fit in with our gypsy heritage; trotting a horse up and down Stewards Lane, but we decided on a fine antique dappled grey rocking horse. Many generations of family and friends had a rock upon it before finally in the late 1980's deciding as family to donate it to the Chelsea and Westminster Hospital for Children. It served a meaningful purpose in our lives and now please let it bring comfort and joy to those children with life challenging illnesses. Intuitive kindness is direct from the heart and the question never arose of its monetary value.

Chapter Two

The Renaissance Kid

The Surrey Lane Estate upbringing was where the non-judgmental consciousness arose in me and where character and personality was born. Likewise, a strong inner will when life challenged me. Contemplating this now, the principles and values of the estate would be a true blueprint for an egalitarian society, a cooperative community where everyone cared for each other in a respectful way. It did not matter your colour, creed, religious inclination. It was all about togetherness; community is unity and it created strength within us all. Yes, many had faults but their virtues outweighed the shortcomings. On the Surrey Lane it wasn't a matter of 'choice' we just had a collective togetherness.

Our new home, 18 Sandcroft Court 170 Battersea Bridge Road SW11 3AJ was one the many new estates after the slum clearances of the 1950's and 1960's. This heralded a new dawn of social cohesion into the 1970's. Our maisonette (French meaning small house) was very modern compared to where we lived previously. It had three good sized bedrooms, toilet upstairs and downstairs and hot air central heating. The latter did result in a lot of damp problems to the extent that residents had to take the council to court. This tale I shall tell later on in my story. We had drying rooms for the laundry and estate shops but when we moved there these had not been completed. There were play areas for the kids and out of our back window was the little red square with its pyramid concrete shape structure and brick wall on the perimeter top; our very own of Hadrian's Wall. This reminds me of a funny story that a classmate had and that I could really relate to. He was asked by the teacher to give the geographical location of Hadrian's Wall. The dialogue went something like this,

'What's geographical mean Miss'?
'The area of the country'
our classmate pondered for a second,
'Miss, Hadrian's Wall is around Adrian's garden'.

The class all erupted into laughter but I could hear sense in his logic. Let's get back on track. The pyramid structure also had a metal slide which was used eventually to ride down our bikes and skateboards. The great application for our replica of the Mayan pyramids was its perfect dimensions as a ramp and take off point for our daredevil Evil Knievel bike stunts.

We had used all furniture and most fittings from the old property because money was tight. Only Dad was at work doing nights as a bulk mail delivery lorry driver for the post office. Mum was the chief guardian in the upbringing of sister and me. We had a black and white television and only half a carpet in the big living room because this was a hand me down from Crampton House. A green vinyl covered three piece suite which, if you had a bit of a sweat on, made your back become attached as if Velcro fastened you to the chair. No telephone, but to us as a family material things were meaningless. A brand new home, no need for a coal bunker, a new adventurous chapter in our lives and we had each other. We moved around the Christmas of 1971. I would be attending my new school, Bolingbroke, which was named after Henry St John 1st Viscount Bolingbroke. He was a politician, government official and political philosopher. As leader of the Tories he supported the Church of England politically despite his anti-religious views and opposition to theology. He was a fervent supporter of the Jacobite rebellion of 1715 thus for him to escape to France meant treason but this was reversed and that was his good fortune. Lord Bolingbroke was Battersea born when Battersea was in the parish of Surrey. His head laid to rest back where he was born and the narrative of his life resonates with mine and the Battersea motto, 'NON MIHI, NON TIBI, SED NOBIS', (neither for myself, nor yourself, but for us). Today some have taken this meaningful motto and translated it as 'not for you, not for me, but for us'. If you look at the notable historical figures of the area they made a social impact on many of the true Battersea folk. This social conscience, expressed as fairness and equality, is encoded into all of us; if only we learn to listen to it over the selfishness of our attachments.

I was only in the infants for a year and half, which had much more to do with playing than learning. Upon graduating to the junior part of the school I really did enjoy the new experience dealing with numbers and especially letters and words. Miss Beck, my teacher, had a 'Purdy' haircut, reddish brownish in colour and as soon as she spoke she had the attention of the class. About this time, coming up to seven, I was really getting into my football. My dream was to be like Peter Osgood, Chelsea's star centre forward, whom I did so meet later on in my life when playing for The Bill police series celebrity eleven football team. As I worked as one of the vehicle coordinators, I had the honour to play a Peter Osgood X eleven with Glenn Hoddle in the side; but again this will be a tale told later on in my series of chronicles. At school I was not the best shape to be a centred forward, more like Billy Bunter with speed akin to a sloth. After an unremarkable centre forward performance Mr. Brian Jones, a wonderful teacher, said '*Stephen I think we have the makings of a quality young goalkeeper here*', as he asked me to shoulder barge him in the corridors of school knocking the wind out of him and with a wry smile upon his face it was a nice way of saying let's put the fat kid in goal because no one else wants to play there. But I am going to say the essence of why I love the written word and storytelling is the series of Peter and Jane English language early readers children's books using the key word reading scheme. The books were designed as materials for teaching a young child to read, using a system of key phrases and words devised by a teacher William Murray. Murray was an educational adviser at borstal and later headmaster of a school for the 'educationally subnormal' as it was termed at the time (to the rest of us street kids we took it to mean 'thick'). From research undertaken in the 1950's with professor Joe McNally, an educational psychologist at the university of Manchester, Murray realised that only twelve words account for a quarter of the vocabulary used in everyday speaking, reading and writing in the English language. Likewise, a hundred words for half the vocabulary and three hundred words for three–quarters, and these books are still used as a teaching aid in nurseries, preschools and kindergartens.

Goalkeeping to me is a natural instinctive anticipatory art, with the aim to read the minds of the opposition and not once have I found difficult to do. Don't worry I did not have this depth of philosophical understanding when I first started playing seriously in goal at seven years old. As I had a secret desire to become a goalkeeper my Grandfather Tom English took me to the Peter Bonetti goalkeeper school, a little earlier than my school teacher persuaded me, and the seed had already been planted maybe a year before. Off I went to Dunkelman's sports shop Falcon Road Battersea to get my goalkeeping attire. But where everyone had green goalie jerseys I decided yellow top, green shorts and yellow socks. The reason I wanted to be different was due to these being the only top and shorts that would fit my podgy frame. I also got Peter Bonetti green gloves which were the 'in thing' of the day, but nowadays would be used for gardening. The Sunday had arrived to go Chelsea FC training ground located in Bishopsford Road Mitcham, a stone's throw from my grandparents' house in Morden. There were not as many as I expected, but Mr. Bonetti was there in person giving us individual coaching catching hand positions, etc. These were the techniques and fundamentals of goalkeeping. I was aged six and the mind was still open to taking in all the necessary information. At this age children are very connected to the internal world, shown by daydreams and imaginative states, and not spoilt by critical or over rational thinking. So what I was taught that day just sunk deep into my subconscious mind which was still like a sponge. My hypothesis is that is why I never found goalkeeping a challenge, it was just there; learned in a habitual pattern into the subliminal mind at the goalkeeping school.

School lessons were great whilst I was learning. As soon as the content changed into multiple choice and copying out of reference books the Dodger mind wandered back into daydream land. I have a lifelong friend who has been a teacher for thirty years and told me that when a teacher fails to recognise the uniqueness of Dodger's way of thinking then they brand the student 'indifferent'. My later secondary education was labeled an unwillingness to learn and being lazy, don't worry Battersea County Secondary School will be getting the full force of my two penneth of knowledge and wisdom since that excruciating five years of tortuous education.

My first foray into being between the posts properly was when I was about eight or nine years old; playing for Bolingbroke School first team when I was a year below everyone else. Battersea Park ashes (where Bob Marley played football in 1977 whilst living in Oakley Street just over Albert Bridge when recording his album 'Exodus') was my Stamford Bridge of the time. Not 4G or Astroturf, yes you heard right ashes, red cinder material which speedway and stock car racing was held on at the now defunct Wimbledon Stadium. I was in the third year of primary and not ecstatic about academia. By this age we had learned to read and write and had some fundamental numerical awareness, so in reality football became an inner love. We had some good players all from the surrounding estates, Surrey Lane and Somerset being the majority of the intake of pupils. I loved goalkeeping because you did not have to run about the pitch, only the area of the eighteen-yard box when needed to sprint out of your goal to perplex the incoming centre forward, like a jousting without horses. Nine times out of ten the battle was won and this was for two reasons. The first was that I was very nifty for a fat kid over eighteen yards and the second was that the attacker must have thought if that fat goalie makes contact with me, he is going to squash me. Already unbeknown to me my talents between the sticks had been spotted by two of the other school's teachers, Mr. Jones of Chesterton and Mr. Marwood (The Revd. Canon Tim Marwood). Both schools also played in the Battersea Schools League, and these chaps happened to be the Battersea District Schools joint managers. This meant if you were picked you would be representing the borough of Battersea at primary school level.

We were not a well-funded school by any standards, just working class kids; 'Fenn Street' kids (from the TV programme 'Please Sir') who were condition to be factory fodder (think of the material of the comedian Mickey Flanagan and you will know what I mean). Amongst my school friends, some had achievable academic intentions. However, the majority could not give a toss, as the combination of fate and limited social mobility meant few fulfilling career opportunities. The teachers were great but I never felt from a personal observation that they instilled an inner belief or confidence that we could achieve any desired career. The majority of my schooling was about qualifications. Creativity was being suppressed and a life of unexcitable employment was on the jaded horizon. I believe that everyone has an innate talent and it is being wasted. The future meant a symbolic gold watch and a state pension where you would have to live a frugal life to make ends meet.

Chapter Three

The Estate on the Battersea Bridge Road

I have always wondered why our area, especially north Battersea, had a relationship to the word Surrey. This included our estate The Surrey Lane, a road running down one side of the estate named Surrey Lane and previous incarnations of schools called Surrey Lane. This goes back to when Battersea Common Fields (before Battersea Park was envisaged) came under the parish of Surrey at that time. If you can imagine Battersea Common Fields in those days was no different to the fields of the south downs of Hampshire, east and west Sussex. These were market gardens created by the fleeing Hugonauts. The purpose of these were to supply the rich and the nobility of London with their fresh fruit and vegetables, now known as the city of London. Battersea Common fair was a place of undesirables and outcasts from society. They included gypsies, travellers trading their ware, punch ups, cock fighting, rule less but soaked in fullness; richness and realness to the common man in that day and age.

My balcony on the Surrey Lane was filled with smells of a global Convent Garden of the time. Our next door neighbour was a Ghanaian princess; the husband was exporting car parts to his country in the 70's long before the commercialization of shipping containers. He used to bundle up his tyres on balcony, but no one took any notice. We had a Jamaican family that my grandad always gave the mackerel we caught when we went sea fishing. The next day the unmistakable fragrance of soused mackerel emanated along the balcony. Then there were the descendants of an Irish family who in winter months made stobhach Gaelach (old Irish stew). To add to the symphony of culinary smells and fare from around the world, a traditional fish and chip shop aroma coming from the local chippie in the row of shops adjacent to our block of maisonettes.

The Surrey Lane was filled with nationalities from all corners of the world. Just to name a few these included Spanish, Greek, Scottish, Jamaican, Trinidadian, Irish (northern and southern), Welsh, Cypriot, Indian, Pakistani, Nigerian and Italy. In my last two years of primary school, I wanted to marry my beautiful jet-black haired teacher Miss Buchannan but I do not think she would have waited for me to grow up. She had one parent who was Chinese and she taught me to say 'Happy New Year' in Cantonese (Gung hay fat choy) and I still remember to this day. On reflection, you can come off a council estate and be bilingual, well at least in one phrase!

The Lane was full of maisonettes and tower blocks. Three bedroom, four bedroom, two bedroom in the tower blocks, the majority twenty floors with one block 13 floors high. The old gits block had single bedrooms that now, as Battersea has been gentrified, are called apartments. When I was growing up, the 'Lane' was called 'notorious' though now locally 'desirable'. It's ironic that ninety four percentage of the estate is privately owned by lawyers, solicitors etc. when in my day the only time solicitors were on the estate was to act on behalf and give legal advice to one of their clients! It was a beautiful place to evolve. We had run outs, tin tan tommy, British bulldog and sick-dying-dead. This last was a game with a tennis ball in the small red square were the aim was to hit another person with the ball and then they became sick. Three direct hits and you were dead and out of the game, but vice versa you could catch the ball and the thrower would become sick; a sort of forerunner to Dodgeball (no pun intended) before the Americans made a sport, spectacle and all day event out of it.

A memory that is always rich in happiness and pleasure was my parents' commitment to providing for us and having a two-week holiday every summer; even though the financial situation was not one of unlimited funds. We had the time of our lives with vacations upon the British shores before we ventured abroad.

Selsey Bill was our first place of adventure. Selsey is a headland on the south coast in west Sussex and the southernmost town in Sussex and at the end of the Manhood Peninsula. It is a former fishing village evolving into an area of many caravan sites which were originally owned by the Bunn family who also owned the world famous all England show jumping course.

Uncle Fred with the wooden leg (Peggy) was my great uncle Fred Cook. He accompanied us on our travels to the south coast, a tailor by trade, he always wore a fedora hat. He was a teacher of my wayward vocabulary at a very young, because if I said 'arsehole' he would give me an opal fruit sweet as a reward! He was a great family member who survived two world wars and enhanced my character.

West Sands caravan park was our venue of choice with its nighttime entertainment in the embassy club. Every night we had some sort of entertainment like the resident band. They had a lady singer who was murdering a song one fateful night. I tried to catch my Mums attention, who happened to be on the other side of the room, 'Mum, Mum' at the top of my voice, 'she sounds like the singing dog' as I pointed to the poor singer. Let's say my folks were not too happy. The audience was in uproar, because the joke was in reference to a scene which was on the Goodies TV show, a wonderful abstract comedy series of the 1970's. Everyone watched it and so understood my sentiments. I was only five but was swiftly ejected from the club by my own parents. They did this with bouncer style credentials and marched back with a purpose of showing them up you little sod, back to the caravan without my nightly burger from less than hygienic or glamorous burger van; so no food poisoning for me then! The burger vehicle owner, whilst cooking the burger with the colour of hands of a mechanic who had just finished a service on a Vauxhall Viva, had fag ash tip as long as a human keratin horn just waiting to fall on the burger which was soaked in lard to add a bit of flavour.

Our next journey to holiday pastures new was a long drive to Paignton in Devon, one hundred and thirty seven miles as the car drives. We had a Hillman Minx estate boasting a top speed of eighty three miles an hour and 26 mpg. This was an overnight journey as dad was use to driving at night because he did not want us to waste a day. The next year, same destination, different vehicle, extra passenger. The car on this visit was a Ford Zephyr four, column change , bench front seats, beautiful motor, and the extra passenger was my Mums Mum, Nanny Lizzy James. She was still grieving the recent loss of her husband George Grandad James. Nanny Liz only passed away in 2002, reaching a ripe old age of 93. She was a little women in stature but did not take any crap from anyone being one of eleven children. She had nine brothers and along with Aunt Ada was one of two sisters. Aunt Ada married a Canadian GI during WW2, and moved to Canada, frequently visiting when she became a widow, and stayed with Nanny Lizzie but got on nerves. Fear always erupted when Aunt Ada visited because someone always dropped dead. Nanny Liz lived near us on the Patmore and I would go and visit her and in all the years I never once witnessed my Nanny James cook a single meal. She would say, '*here are Stephen John*', she always called me that, '*go up Harrington's Wandsworth Road and get yourself some pie and mash*'. To Londoners, pie mash and liquor is the food of the gods. Later on in her life we were able to get her a move to be closer to her three daughters, Aunt Bet, Aunt Maureen and my Mum. Nanny Liz was at Falcon Road Battersea not too far from Clapham Junction which should really be called Battersea Junction, as when the railways came into Battersea they did not want the working class stereotype on their spanking new railway station. I was always visiting my Nanny James right up to her passing. The conversation always went '*hello Stephen John, popover love to Greggs and get us a couple of sausage rolls and whatever you want, and while you're out pop down the high street (Battersea) and put a bet on for us, hurry up the first race is at two*'. Liz loved a bet, could have gone to higher education but grandad Cook would not pay the fees; at times a very negative and limited expectation of staying within your class. Paignton was a delightful seaside resort, cream teas and jam, a fractional intake of calories in the English reckoning! It was not too commercialised at this time, quoted as the English Riviera, we always were exploring as a family. Once we went to the Plymouth seawater lido with Nanny Liz in tow, my sister and I moved Nans deckchair because of her disdain of direct sunlight, and Lizzy did like a moan. I think I have carried on that family trait. We were moving the deckchair with the urgency of two people doing a demonstration of an exercise gym item on QVC the digital Sky shopping channel. On this holiday we were unfortunately in the security of a campsite car park. Dad nobly or foolishly, with a determined attempt to teach my dear Mother to drive,

Dad said 'right get in the car love',

'John', mum said, 'can I ask you a question'

'off course love'

'well how do you drive a car with three pedals with two feet ?'

Dad just replied, 'get out the car love'

and that was the end of my Mother's desire to be Margaret Allan (the original Bentley girl at Brooklands).

Our horizons were extending ever further afield, two hundred and fifty five miles to be exact, Battersea to Newquay; let the good times roll. This was 1976 the year of the infamous drought, oh boy was it hot. Dad's first task was to drop off my sister and her two friends at Paddington train station and we would meet up again after our lengthy drive. Dad as the driver, Mum as the navigator whose map reading skills were quite brilliant. In rallying terms dad was Stig Blomqvist and mum the co-driver Bjorn Cederburg. If Mum said turn left, we turned left, even if it was the wrong way, a collective misdirection. Still both Dad and I have an issue every now and then when we go around a roundabout countless times, misplacing the exit which extends our journey. Newquay (Tewynblustri was its Cornish former name) was an absolutely outstanding town on the north coast of Cornwall, in the south west of England. A former fishing port on the north Atlantic coast, the resort is widely regarded as the surf capital of the UK with Fistral Beach which has a reputation as one of the best beach breaks in Cornwall. We were all staying together in a bed and breakfast residence at Porth Bean road Newquay where the thoroughfare meandered to a stunning beach.

The place of choice for our sun and sea most days was Newquay Harbour adjacent to a magnificent beach, with an ebb and flow of seawater that revealed nature's beauty in all her glory. It had a stretch of unspoilt sand and when the tide was at its lowest it was an ideal area for fun and frolics; but behold don't try to jump off the harbour at such periods otherwise your overall height would greatly be reduced because alas no water just sand! Beware also of the lesser weaver fish which habitually buries itself in the sandy shallow waters. At low tide it is prone to be stepped on by us intelligent species when the little fellow is just minding its own business. It can cause various symptoms of illness, and I have witnessed many an individual screaming in discomfort. We 'plotted up' (our term for a base camp!) by the harbour and beach for its access to various food outlets and convenience facilities. Importantly also was it for changing swimming gear after a long day with granules of sand in every province of bare flesh.

In those days the Newquay Harbour had a wonderful character for a harbour master, who was forever bellowing the rules and regulations of the aforementioned area *'GET OFF THE HARBOUR WALL'* in his Cornish lilt. We had wonderful conversations about his time serving the country as a naval man in WW2, you would be talking and then you would still see his eyes scanning the kingdom of his domain. And he definitely was the king waiting for some foolhardy soul to dare to walk on the summit of his kingdoms wall. Mid-sentence he would lock onto someone resembling a radar saying *'GET OFF THE HARBOUR WALL'*, and then just carry on the conversation.

Out of the harbour there were a many fishing boat trips, hour long, feathers on a hand line searching for mackerel. Now being still quite young age, I had to be accompanied by an adult and Mum insisted that Dad took me (in reality he did not have a choice). Dad has never had the best sea legs; the boats on the boating lake at Battersea Park are a bit too much for him. However, he was brave and foolhardy and would accompany his son on this voyage of the unknown. Dad was Nelson and I was Hardy. Dad's ropey sea legs go back to a deep sea fishing trip out of Littlehampton years back. This happened along with many Battersea old school characters and to say the sea was rough was an understatement. From the point out of the River

Arun causeway to the time he returned, my dad was throwing up projectiles both out on the sea surface and the interior of the boat; similar to a Jackson Pollock painting. This, our hour trip, in fact should have been a plan sailing but as soon as the boat chugged along out of the confines and smoothness of the harbour water, into the open waters of the Atlantic sea, a colour of hulk green came over his face and my poor dad was sea sick for the whole hour. I did catch plenty of mackerel, which I gave to the stray cats free of charge in a cut up state. So I am glad we were inner city dwellers otherwise if my dad's only source of income was as a trawler man, we would have starved.

The one definite I can safely say about our family is that we adore our grub (food). When you visit Cornwall the true taste of the county is the Cornish pasty. It should not need resuscitating like the flat sort you get in regularly fish and chip shops where they look as if in production someone as purposely taken all the air out, nicked some of the meat, and rationed the vegetables. Cornish pasties built in the shire are a proper job and we all consumed one a day, every day. Hank Marvin (starving) after a morning trying to be The Duke (Duke Kahanamoku the father of surf) on a belly board where my skill levels had not yet develop to a upright standing position. My weight distribution, mass and fat anchored me to the belly board whilst filling my imagination was The Hawaii Five-0 theme song (and Steve McGarrett the ultra-cool detective of the TV series to be a composed surfer)! In reality I was having more wipe outs than the number of times the Beach Boys their songs played. However, I did find a Laurel to my Hardy in the shape a skimboard (big water frisbee). You ran parallel to the waves breaking to the shallow part of the beach and launch the board on water frisbee style. Then you run after it, jump on it and just skim along. After many attempts of face planting myself into the sea and sodden sand, the fat boy, the grockle (out of towner) had accomplished a fair standard to the endeavor; so all the pain was worth the experience.

I had taken notice that on kids grapevine that skateboards were in the ascendance so when we use to stroll through the town near to Newquay train station I noticed a surf shop with a few of these new skateboards in the window. There was a yellow slalom board for £12.99 so after constant sulking and whining my folks purchased the skateboard. In my heart it felt as if Christmas day had come despite it being the hottest period on record (It was 1976 and the year of punks and rebellion in the middle of the South West of England). To ride a skateboard successfully you do need just a little instruction if you have never ridden one before and suitably forgiving surfaces help. But not me the Master of Chaos, The Battersea crusader, I decide that I was going to start my schooling on Porth Bean Road which had a deceptive slope. So I, brain of Britain, decided in my infinite wisdom this is where I should first test it out and not for one moment listening to the guidance of my parents. My first and only attempt at being Tony Hawkes (famed skateboarder), was where the board went down Porth Bean Road without me! I went to put my foot down to step on the board but as no physical weight landed, my new pride and joy scuttled off down the lane on its own accord turning potential energy into kinetic energy and whizzed off and collided with a wall besides the road. This reflected the error of my ways and I could have been hurt. If mystically, somehow, I already could have been an accomplished skateboarder I would have ridden the wave. My next swift, intuitive decision after my Mother swore at me, was to place the new, not broken yet, skateboard in the car and waited till we got back to the concrete jungle of the Surrey Lane. There, nearly every surface was flat because it was all pavements, great thinking Dodger, and on my return from my expedition south-west, I was one of the first kids on the estate to have obtained a skateboard. I did actually become quite an average rider, win, win, moral here, listen to your parents, they know you. Finally, I did come back from Newquay with something unexpected and that was ringworm! I went back to school with scabs on my face akin to me having just returned from a leper colony.

Chapter Four

Waiting for Dodgot

I Love acting. It is so much more real than life
(Oscar Wilde)

My first virgin performance and debut on the stage was in a school production of George Orwell's 'Animal Farm'. Again, the leading role was already mine and I did not even have to have an audition. The Teacher, Mr. Guy, our wonderful music teacher who created the music and lyrics for the play had already shoehorned me in to play Napoleon the leader/dictator of the animals. Unbeknown to me I really did not want to be an actor or act as I had set my desires on being in the choir. However, my dulcet tones were not conducive to the choir's projection of vocal perfection. I was unable to harmonise in unison with the rest of the singers, as Mr. Guy said, *'Stephen your character and personality is much better suited to acting than singing'*. In truth my voice was monotone with the added annoyance of someone scratching their nails down a blackboard. I am an introvert and extrovert both. I love people because they teach many lessons that we need to learn about ourselves but I also love my quietude and solitude. In truth, I have anti-social periods where I'm a miserable git, so putting myself on a stage to perform scared me but also excited.

The first hurdle to overcome was the thick script of dialogue. I had to learn for the play, which I had a month to do with rehearsals in between. It included learning the brilliant songs Mr. Guy had written to give profound meaning to the performance. Orwell's creation and his leanings towards social democracy, his political philosophy, is a good metaphor description for the state of humanity and society in the present day. At times in modern society it feels no difference to the plight of the Topuddle Martyrs. These were six agricultural labourers from the village of Topuddle, Dorset, England who in 1834 were convicted of swearing a secret oath as the members of the friendly society of agricultural labourers. Really, they were the first trade unions in a dispute against the cutting of wages. A local landowner grassed them up and this, in turn, united the men who then became more powerful. As a result, government produced an obscure dictatorial law to stop this uprising of the working man. Even further back the peasants revolt across large parts of England in 1381, where the peasants again where being treated crap by the landowners and thought, leave it out, we are not having it. The peasants revolt was fed by the economic and social upheaval of the 14th century. A more modern illustration is the Jarrow marches of 1936 and was organised as a crusade of protest against the unemployment and poverty suffered in the Tyneside town. Even more recent an example was the miners' strikes where Maggie Thatcher 'the milk snatcher' closed down all the collieries. The miners (peasants) were fighting against their livelihood being taken away and the future for generations to come. Now all these former colliery towns have high unemployment and higher than average mental health issues. It is just the same with some of our ship building cities and towns. Is there a theme here? Do we buy everything abroad cheaper? And does it lack quality of workmanship reflecting a loss of artisan skills? Our British car industry once led the world but between the bosses and the sixteen different unions allowed the collapse, resulting in the metaphorical burning of Rome. So the bosses fiddled like Nero while British automobiles died on their wheels. Right folks, now I will get off my imaginary Hyde Park Corner speakers plinth and get on with my chronicles.

The afternoon world or at least southwest London premier of Bolingbroke's school production was upon me. My wardrobe was made up of a crap brown polo neck and a pair of brown corduroy trousers from Walters of Falcon Road Battersea. I was shaking like someone with DT"s but as the production began, I felt a sense of this is going to be OK. Joining in with the choir singing,

'All animals are equal, but some are more equal than others,
On a cold grey misty morning and the animals are all asleep,

The wind blows through the tree tops and there is hardly enough to eat,
But we are down on Animal farm, for another season we will have our reasons,
When animal farmers were made'

Mr. Guy's thought provoking lyrics had a poignant message. As an 11 year old it goes totally over your head but there was a crescendo of '*bravos*' all over the school hall as the curtain went down. The blinds went up on the assembly hall windows to let a bit of light on the subject and was followed by great applause from the audience, teachers, parents and pupils. Whilst there was no Oscar or Bafta for me the experience was absolutely wonderful and this became an achievement I never thought I could have, but I did!

Chapter Five

I am the Goalkeeping Paradox

The school year is 1976/77 and Bolingbroke Primary School football team will win the Battersea Schools League for the first time in many years. I go on to represent Battersea Schools District and it is the first time that players are represented from different cultural backgrounds. I also play the lead performance of Napoleon the pig in George Orwell's 'Animal Farm' (Allegorical Novella). At the time, this was a controversial play to be performed by 10 and 11 year olds. Last year of primary school, I still had desire that Miss Buchannan would want to marry me when i was older. If this was The Graduate, I was Dustin Hoffman but a bit younger. My education and insight of the female gender at that time, was women dressed in bras and knickers in the Freemans catalogue or Maria Morgan on 'A Handful of Songs' (the children's sing-along music TV show). School at this stage was offering a repetitive mindset and forever telling us that without qualifications we can achieve nothing in life. This then was programming a subconscious fear of failure if we did not listen to what was being taught. In my mind I was always thinking 'bollocks' and ' I want to do things I enjoy, love'. I wanted to learn valuable life lessons and skills from my own experience. I desired an adventurous life like my Grandfather Tom English. instilled within me, not just be non-thinking algorithm mindset, who becomes a sheep, not a shepherd, subservient consciousness of the educational system, where grades were of utmost importance and my imagination and creativity, abstract thinking was not or would never be recognised or nurtured, schooling should not tell us what to think, but how to think (just my observation). I had fashioned my way (Dodged) to be the chair monitor and put the vinyl on the dansette record player for hymns (when a Knight won his spurs, Morning as broken etc.). As the morning assembly monitor, rousing hymns along with my life great long friend, who I sat next to in class, my friend was fantastic at maths and would lovingly help with mathematical issues I was having. I copied his work, he lived on the Surrey Lane, and we played schools, district, and youth football together, and are still in contact after nearly 46 years. This was a friendship cemented in childhood, and although we have taken very different life paths, we share ethics, principles and values in common. These were instilled at a young age and I believe they resonate with us. The most important life messaging are introduced in childhood by the wise of generations past as they participate in our upbringing. For someone to be a good quality goalkeeper the body dimensions have to be of slender persuasion rather than the rotund nature of my shell; a juvenile Michelin man springs to mind. However, for someone of this stature I was unbelievable agile, nimble and quick (well at least off the 18 yard line) and lively; a paradox of the label of what a goalkeeper should look like.

The Battersea Park ashes were my Trafalgar and the HMS victory for my battles was the goal. My arms, legs and every part on this fine figure of a lad were cannons. With all of my inner will and desire, I would block or stop any of the French or Spanish armada (opposition team players) from scoring or winning. I would be as nimble as a butterfly dancing in the wind but did not end up having my kiss me hardy (Dodger) moments when the war (game) was won. I received many battle scars every week; too right! I had elbows, knees scratched to shreds, by Tuesday or Wednesday after the Saturday game. There were little pockets of poison festering out of the scabs and Mum, with her tough love approach, just put some TCP on it whilst saying that it would be fine. Thinking of it now, putting TCP on repairing wounds is a sort of self-flagellation, but it did work and heal.

Every Saturday morning Mum and I were up early whilst Dad was in bed after his night at work driving. Breakfast, get in my goalkeeping kit, and meet my friend and his younger brother, by the shops down stairs. Us three boys, and the volunteer chaperone, Mum, Eileen English would take a gentle stroll through the Ethelburga Estate and 10 minute walk to Battersea Park for kick off time 9:30am. Every Saturday through the football season this was our life and routine. It was only for school football cup semi-finals, final and district trials that we were allowed on the hallowed turf of Battersea Park grass or the nice pitch by the fountains left over from the 1953 festival of Britain (that was held partially at Battersea Park). The fountains were the free lido in the hot summer months and water borne diseases were the furthest from our minds. Rather we were taken to falling down the V-shaped gullies and stubbing toes on the noughts and crosses grid of the endless pipes for the fountains to operate. Everyone's towels laid down around the fountains thinking we were holidaying in the south of France.

The day of the trials had arrived and we were on the sacred pitch adjacent to the fountains. There was dog poo aplenty and many trialist were there from all the Battersea primary schools. These included Latchmere, Chesterton, John Burns, Sacred Heart, Heathbrook, John Milton, Shaftesbury Park, Wix's Lane and Sir James Barrie (which was my old school) just to name a few. Their school team football managers put the trialists forward and I cannot speak highly enough of these teachers. My personal experience told me that the problem lay with the educational system rather than the teachers. Mr. Brian Jones, our deputy head teacher and manager, had put forward another lad from our school called Ian and myself for the trial. There were boys everywhere, Mr. Jones and Mr. Marwood, joint managers of the district team (the Brain Clough and Peter Taylor of their day) set the trials in motion. They chose two teams of boys, I think we all had our school kits on, so you had to remember who was on your team. I was not chosen so was on the sidelines, the subs bench, and felt dejected but with hope in my heart that I would get on later in the game. The first half finished, players were selected for the second half, but again I was not chosen and so my spirit was starting to crumble. I could feel the bottom lip starting to quiver, I am suffering from upset syndrome, and in a minute I am going to cry. I thought to myself that I am going to have to pluck up the courage and audacity to ask Mr. Jones when I was going to play in my beloved goal. I practised in my mind a few times, and thought right it's now or never fatboy! *'Sir, Sir, Mr. Jones, Sir when am I going to play Sir'?* I was waiting for a stern look, but instead Mr. Jones spun round and said ' *Don't worry English Boy you're already in, no need for you to play, we know your talent, we're just finding out who is going to be your number two*'. Mr. Marwood would always greet my Grandfather Tom with a salute to his cap, and an assertive 'MR ENGLISH'. The only difference, from the reserve keeper and myself, apart from a few stone, was when a powerful shot was aimed, he would pat it down to take the sting out of the shot, where I wouldn't hesitate to take the rock hard mitre size 3 football straight into my 'midriff' and thus have control of the situation. That was the distinction between the two Battersea junior district school representative goalkeepers of the season 1976/77.

Bolingbroke were well on the way to winning the league. I played for the school the previous year and became aware of this little bald gentleman stand behind my goal and talk to me. Now, I knew he was not a weirdo, because his son played for Chesterton School but was a year higher than I was. One day he started a conversation, *'you're Dodger English?'* I thought how the hell does he know my name? Then he asked if I played Sunday youth football? After saying no he asked, *'would you like too?'* I said *'I don't really know you better ask my Mum'*, who was on the sidelines watching the game. This went on for quite a while, then one of the Mums of one of the other team's starting talking to my Mum. An under 11's youth team had started and would like me to come and join them. My Mum's reply was always *'it's up to Dodger if he wants to play'*. My parents never forced me to do anything. The little bald chap was a man named Freddie Ball, a lifelong friend whom I now tower over like Gulliver (he is one of the Lilliput little people). He is a Battersea man through and through. He was a youth leader/worker at a local youth club called Caius which formed in 1887. Some undergraduates and fellows from Gonville and Caius College Cambridge rented a house in Battersea and started a college settlement where former undergraduates from the college lived and ran a range of clubs for local residents. Shortly after they started a very successful boys club and later a girls club and found it attracted members from the poorest and least educated young in the area. In 1886 Edward Wilson, a Gonville and Caius graduate came to London as a medical student to be a 'settler' at Caius house and to help with the youth club. Edward was later to be the Doctor on Captains Scott's expedition to the North Pole and to die with him in 1912 on the return journey. Caius had always a great reputation for boxing talent including Peter Waterman brother of and Dennis (actor, Sweeney, Minder) and producing worthy pugilists. Peter was a welterweight champion. The lady who was in conversation with my Mum was Rita Ennor whose son Dean played for Heathbrook and Battersea with me. George, husband and dad, was the manager of the new Caius under 11 team and they wanted me to be their goalkeeper. So after some convincing because I was a bit of a wally, Myself, Ian and Ian's brother Lawrence signed up to play for Caius. This was without doubt the best decision of my childhood and youth.

Chapter Six

The Village Brings Up the Child

The entire community must interact with children for those children to grow in a safe and healthy environment. This comes from my interpretation of an African proverb (Nigerian Igbo culture) meaning that the villagers look out for the child and its upbringing belongs to the community. This is the case regardless of the child's biological upbringing; this was the Surrey Lane, this was Battersea.

As I have said, we come from an extremely large extended family and with my Mum's recent passing one of her many cousins rang to offer his condolences. He told me a tale of my Nanny Ivy English, about a period just after WW2. They were all living in Latchmere Grove in Battersea and for nearly all of the families money was tight. There were many young children down the Grove and he said that Aunt Ivy would round up all the kids, maybe 30, and buy every single one an ice cream. It may not seem a lot in the materially driven world we live in now, but back then ration books were in circulation; my Dad still scorns when margarine is mentioned. Few children had Christmas presents of note and my Dad said he only remembers his Dad making his

Christmas gifts. However, the essence was of unconditional love and the community was one.

I believe these ethical principles and values were apparent for most parents who lived on the estate and surrounding areas. The majority of families only had one parent in employment, so belts had to be tightened. Any excessive outlay was not tolerated and if you could not afford it you didn't buy it. If needed the item was bought. I clearly remember once my parents had bought me these beautiful pair of gola getaways (trainers) and after my constant playing football for a week I had started to wear the tread pattern on the bottom of the trainers. I got extremely upset, not that my folks had told me off, but because my Dad had to work nights to give us little bits of material comfort. I didn't mean to but I totally disrespected his commitment to provide for his family.

My red Mk2 Raleigh Chopper, a Christmas present I think in 1974, was my adaptation of the classic award winning short film 'The Red Balloon' created by Albert Lamorisse. Made in 1956 this was a French fantasy, comedy-drama featurette. Like Pascal, the boy who finds the balloon, I had a simple love and friendship with my chopper and nearly five decades later I still have my red chopper, waiting patiently to be restored and loved once more.

Back then a chopper in your possession was the holy grail of bicycles, and I had one; symbolically akin to a wife I never had (although I was a bit young to tie the knot!). At times we would fight, or she would teach me not to be a show off like the time I tried to stand up on the pedals to ride faster, full body heaviness on the pedals, my foot slipped down to the shin which had hardly any skin. It was a crash course to connect, full blow, as it grated most of that snare drum width skin of my shin. And then in that moment, the foot losing its balance, pain number two as it proceeded to let my nether regions collide with the 3 gear T piece gear change (metal and plastic) of my angry red chopper! Causing extreme pain both in the shin and the nuts (testicles) I dismounted the red chopper and had to hop and dance like a tribal Cherokee calling on the rain. This was accompanied with the high-pitched voice of someone who had taken a great big gulp of helium. Though comparable to quarrelling lovers, the liaison with my red chopper was still the apple of eye.

My chopper and I went everywhere and did everything together and was my first platonic love. I could do twenty-one pavement wheelies pulled in 1st gear, ramps built on the grass round the back of Fraser court, with Cramner and Compton house opposing height either side of the arena resembling the twin towers of the original Wembley Stadium. The daredevil or daft push bike stunt kids in demand, the ramp was constructed of an old paneled door and Unigate milk crate which was borrowed from Ernie the milkman. The fans, kids who were not as fearless or foolish as some of us made up the crowd, persuaded to be the equivalent to the red London Transport buses Robert Evil Knievel used in his infamous Wembley attempt in 1975 to jump into the world record books with a 60, 000 crowd. We had, however, about 11 child spectators plus one adult, Willy the tramp. The way that Willy dressed might today be categorised as like a homeless person, but Willy wasn't homeless he had a flat in Whitgift house one of the tower blocks. He would wander around the estate aimlessly at times but his main place of residence in the daytime hours was on the wall surrounding the flower beds, which in all of my 35 years on the Lane never witnessed any colour, shrubs yes, but alas no flowers. By the shops on the front of Surrey Lane Battersea Bridge Road, he wore two to three layers of clothes even in the summer. A bit of Daz 'whiter than white' would have helped as the colour of his clothes were overcast day grey. He gave off a strange odour, rather than a rancid pong. He never begged, though people coming off the bus at the estate stop would often give him their loose change. He would be straight into the fish and chip shop to get his cod and chips, or if loose change didn't allow then it would be 5 pence worth of crackling. Willy was our Willy, he was our Tramp and he was never judged or ridiculed. Then there was also young Danny Don't Know, we called him that because no one ever knew his surname nor did he. Maybe he had some sort of learning difficulty but it didn't matter, Danny Don't Know was still one of us. He would always volunteer to be the final bus in line of bodies for our ramp jumping stupidity. We had three persons lying down then four persons and I think the most completed was 9 foolhardy souls. This was a jump accomplished by a lesser framed child than myself and the stars of the ramp jumping stunts always played their part by laying down as the imaginary bus. I still have the bike in my garden shed. However, the continuous ramp jumping wear and tear means the only part of my chopper from the Raleigh factory which is not totally original are the handlebars. The new handles were needed as they were snapped whilst attempting a 7 kids jump. I was peddling like the clappers (or a 1960's tour de France rider on amphetamines) in 1st gear up into 2nd gear and I'm flying now like Eddie Merck (or Eddie Large) with legs pumping like pistons on the flying Scotsman steam train. Then approaching the ramp at warp speed for take off! I could not get in third gear because of the lack of landing space and the fact that I had reached my cylinder capacity (cc) in my human internal combustion engine. I hit the ramp square on, took off gracefully, sailed into the air with wind sweeping my strawberry blonde locks back, no crash hat in our days, upon landing cleanly and clearing everyone. My handlebar stem decided to submit finally to the constant pummeling and snapped. Yes, my gonads did receive an unfortunate impact but the long seat of the chopper was quite padded, so no helium voice this time. This was my triumph over adversity as I had my new personal best of seven buses (kids really) and I did not even lay a chopper tyre on Danny Don't Know. I had top mechanic Dad on duty 24 hours, always there to save the day by replacing those broken ramp jumping worn out handlebars. Bloody marvelous. When you were growing in less complicated times everyday was an adventure.

The elders, the adult residents concurred that the estate needed a lobbying co-operation; therefore, the Surrey Lane Estate tenants association was born. There for the residents to help, guide and support young and old. My Mum, because she liked being in charge (a piano playing rather than carrier) was one of the main protagonist in the tenants association and especially to help children and the OAPs. With fees collected, which was minimal so everyone could afford it, there was Christmas time down to the cash and carry to purchase 200 tins of Rover biscuits for the elderly and they were all delivered by the committee members to every over 65 year olds on the estate. There were selection boxes for all the kids and days out to Chessington and the coast.

The first Surrey Lane Youth Club, before our own estate community hall was built, was held in the crypt of the famous St Mary's Church Battersea Church Road. It is amongst the earliest five documented holy sites of land south of the River Thames.

The original church was built around 800AD, and the present church built in 1777. The church has a strong connection with art and literature, with William Blake married there and JMW Turner painting the River Thames from a vestry window. In the crypt, Benedict Arnold's gravestone, an American hero of the revolutionary war who later became the most famous traitor in American history after he switched sides to the British. We were receiving history lessons and we did not know it! Old Benedict's gravestone was a good surface to play penny up; always wondered why there were many yanks always visiting Battersea, getting lost on the Surrey Lane and asking where the church was.

Chapter Seven

Playing Out and Playschemes – All is One!

Unlike the modern younger generation with Xboxes, iPhones, Facebook, twitter, YouTube etc., our world did not revolve around love, likes or shares, or the latest mobile. The nearest we got to mobile communication was two tin cans and a piece of string between them. We played out, actually, we were never indoors, and probably the only night all the family were together was Saturday night watching the Generation Game on the one family television.

We all had a sense of adventure, the red bus rover ticket cost about forty-five pence and you could go on all London transport buses and underground trains for the whole day. Always my first travel plan, whilst being in receipt of a red bus rover, was any bus to Clapham Junction then a 77 to Wandsworth Road to make my first stop in my imaginary orienteering map, Harrington's pie, mash, liquor and stewed eels establishment. There I would have double pie, double mash and double liquor as fuel for my journey all over London. I would visit places like the Science, Natural History and Victoria and Albert museums. I would jump the underground to Piccadilly Circus to go in the famous Lilywhites sports shop, to dream and drool over the next goalkeeping gloves, kit and football boots; what my heart desired. These were halcyon days of yore, halcyon days of youth and a carefree spirit of a wandering star when I lived in the moment. Just simple things create a straightforward life. I always believe the blessing is to have gratitude for just wake up every morning. Even from a young age, I have always had this philosophy. I do not fit in with modern thinking; the powers that be straighten rivers then wonder why it floods!

Battersea Park was our green and pleasant land. I still have fond memories of the funfair with the knock the lady out the bed stall, how contentious would that be in the present day with political correctness; (just a different time, a different generation)? The park keepers in their all brown uniforms were the parks police of the day, but with much more understanding because the majority employed were local residency. However, it didn't stop them chasing you if rules and regulations were not adhered too, especially playing on the rocks by the boating lake or fishing in the stock pond by the pump house. Nevertheless, the escape was always in our favour, because the parkies had the sit up and beg bicycle contraption, with us mischievous little so and so's on our choppers. Once the chase commenced, the three-speed chopper gear change came in very handy. We'd get a good head start and across country into the wooded areas of the park, and finally reaching our exit at the park gate on Albert Bridge Road. This led back to our estate and victory was ours for the moment;

but those parkies, storm trooper like will commence battle again if we dared break the constitution of our green and pleasant land.

I feel a real notion of foreboding, with a sense of despair within society that the vast majority of the younger generation are growing up with a total lack of devoted adults who are prepared to mentor and be positive role models for the many lost souls of adolescence. In my subjective observation, successive governments have lacked meaningful substance to their programme for our youth, with no development of character or personality. They are plastering over the cracks; let's just create another committee with the hundreds of other committees that achieve absolutely nothing, what is the cause? We have to endeavour to get away from a one cap fits all, dotting the I's, crossing the T's fixed mindset; fitting everyone in the same box. A more positive philosophy would be to help, guide and support our youth. A serious look at providing wider opportunities that are not just based on academic prowess would be good a start. It is wisdom that gives rise to community and that creates unity. We are losing too many beautiful and confused young lives through suicide when the challenges of life get tough or through a gang culture, which is the surrogate family. This needs to change! Action speaks louder than words!

The year is 1977, Silver Jubilee, and I'm going from mandatory primary state school offering a fit in a box education to a mandatory secondary school state education where there are more boxes to fit into. Oh well, at least my imagination will get a good work out and where I would learn less than in previous years' schooling. I also became an uncle at 11 years old on the night of 26 April 1977. It will always be a period I will remember with great heartfelt fondness for what was going to happen on this night of my birthday; let's just say it took all and sundry by surprise!

I had finished my season of representing Battersea District Schools football team with winning the Ernest Bevin trophy at Richardson Evans playing fields Roehampton (where the crazy gang of the original Wimbledon FC and Fulham FC went on to have their training facility there). It is now in the ownership and possession of an exclusive school for those that can afford fees and entitlement, after the wide sweeping gentrification of southwest London.

Do you get my drift how things have changed or not? These people were in the 1880's and were the individuals who would go and pay to watch the working classes in their slums such as Hackney doing their everyday jobs, and we are not supposed to be a classless society! We got stuffed For Battersea in the final of the all London Kay cup final played at Finsbury park by East London district. We lost 7-1 and was the most I have let in as a goalkeeper. The other team contained David Kerslake who went on to play professionally for QPR and is now a well-respected football coach. I have only lost two cups in my many appearances and that was one of them.

My inner teacher was always my guide and outside sources, if I believed were true and could benefit my life, I would take on board. But if it didn't make sense, then I was off in my imagination. As the great psychiatrist and psychoanalyst Carl Gustav Jung quotes, *'who looks outside dreams, who looks inside awakes'* (in a letter to Fanny Bowditch on 22nd October 1916).

The 26th of April 1977 will forever be a day that the memories are still fresh as a daisy. I had played for my youth team Caius House under 11 football team in a 5 a side tournament at Kings Georges Park Wandsworth and we so happened to win it. The final went to penalties, and being a five a side goal, was much smaller than the standard youth size. I saved a few penalties in the shoot-out, as my portly frame took up most of the goal and the opposition penalty taker didn't have much of an area to shoot at! So we won the tournament. Mum and I went back to our home on Surrey Lane where my skin and blister (sister) was already indoors as Dad was doing the night shift driving on the Royal Mail.

I went to bed, still excited and full of glorious victorious energy from winning the tournament and it took me a while to drop off to sleep. Not long into my sleep I heard my sister in the upstairs toilet shouting for my Mum at the top of her voice, '*Mum, Mum, come up here quick*'. I heard Mum run up the stairs swearing, go into the bathroom/toilet and let out an almighty scream. Now for my Mum who was tough as anyone I know and always in emotional control, for her to let out this primal howl, in my mind there was something drastically wrong with my Sister in the khazi. Mum then ran down the stairs, out of the front door and went to get Ann, a wonderful lady who lived at the end maisonette at the end of the balcony. So I, Dodger the brave or naive, decided that I would go and investigate the commotion that just occurred in the '*oh dear what can the matter be, something ain't right with Julie in the lavatory*'. I got up and walked along, half asleep on the upstairs landing, to see what the bloody hell was going on. Arriving at the bathroom, I was confronted and then confused by my sister sitting on the bog with a newborn baby in her arms! I'm stood there in my paisley patterned pyjamas, thinking am I in a dream or nightmare and wondering what the hell is going on? The scene was similar to Sweeney Todd's barbershop, claret (blood) everywhere, my Sister with congealed blood all about her person. Mum had disappeared to get help, all I did was put some towels on my parent's bed, help my Sister and newborn nephew on to the bed. I knew it was a boy because I could see his winkle and then I went back to bed. By this time Mum and Ann were back to tackle this very unimaginably surreal situation.

My Dad was at work and was called into the office by a PHG (postman higher grade) to be told, '*Arthur*' (his nickname at work, from the well-known actor of the day Arthur English), '*congratulations you are a granddad*'. To dads bewilderment he said '*me a Granddad*' and the reply confirmed, '*Yes Arthur, your daughter has given birth at home*'. My Sister at the time was still attending the same school as me though in the sixth form, and even on the day of my nephew's birth was in a swimming lesson earlier in the day.

My Sister knew she was up the duff. By an unbelievable inner strength, she told herself she wasn't because she had to focus on getting her A level qualifications. Her dreams of becoming a vet relied on it. My sister was in the Queens Charlotte's hospital being assessed for her mental and physical well-being, which was absolutely fine. Her boyfriend's mum and sister were visiting and just after my Mum and Aunty arrived. My sister's boyfriend's Mum piped up and said, '*Right you can come and live with us, we have sorted out the bedroom to fit the cot in*'. In mid-sentence my Mum said '*no she ain't coming to live with you, she's coming home*'. There was a little bit of a disagreement, my sister in tears, wrong thing to do to take on two Battersea girls, Mum and Aunty. The error of her ways were pointed out by my aunty when she said, 'if you don't shout up, I'll take you out in the corridor and punch you down every flight of stairs'. Now being of a Victorian style hospital that would have hurt considerably. I'm not an advocate of violence, but in my values of life, family is everything. You can see why I never intended to marry a Battersea lass; it would be like marrying your Aunty or Sister. Battersea girls don't take any bull off anyone.

My Nephew arrived home, a great aunt had provided the cot, and Mums cousins a load of clothes.

Aunty, neighbours, cousins, friends on the estate had given everything needed to bring up my nephew meeting all the requirements to aid the child's first months home. Presents were arriving for my sister and new nephew, as I said in one of my other tales, it is the community that brings up the child and this life-changing situation ultimately proves the proverb to be the truth.

With the silver jubilee parties on the horizon, the feeling of a brighter future resonated in the country and the British do love a party and a knees up; a celebration where everyone is supposed to be equal subjects! My final report from Bolingbroke was completed, all good grades, just above average, with my English report saying 'Stephen has an interesting and lively writing style, and is starting to write for pleasure'. How did my primary teachers know? It is a shame that my secondary educational instigators did not nurture my instinctive, flip knows where it comes from ability. My love for my newborn nephew was unconditional and still is this to this day. Mine is a big brother mentality instead of the typical uncle. I am always there for my two nephews, great niece, great nephew, and godchildren and in a way I'm a comfort blanket. I have never been able to give them many materialistic goods but always give absolute time and heart felt love; this is a principle that I extend to all my family and friends.

With the jubilee parties being organised, Mum at the centre as piano player rather than the carrier. She liked pointing and telling others what to do but always in a non-egotistical way. Union Jacks, banners and bunting were hung from every balcony.

The gatherings for all the estate shindigs are taking place within the confines of each maisonettes front areas, which had landscaped areas that were great for dogs to poo. This was highly dangerous when playing cricket in our small red square, fielding on the boundary, just in front of front doors, going for a catch, one hand off the bricked wall of the maisonette. The batsmen would be out, skidding and slipping arse over tit on the dog mess, making the catch, the delight of feeling you were Ian Botham completing a catch for the Ashes. Then, realising and inhaling the load of dog poo on your Woolworth specials. The rancid aroma produced and involuntary heaving, eyes filled with tears. Are you going to honk up or not, with an intensity as if you had drank a bottle of pernod without lemonade? We followed the seasons for our sporting endeavours, football winter, summer cricket and tennis when Wimbledon was on. We had estate drains with their great grid configuration where you could play marbles, not only with shutters, but also with the smaller versions. The objective of the game was to get your marble on the oppositions drain grid line, alternate go's, winning the oppo's marble if you did so.

The day was upon us, everyone doing his or her bit to help the setting up of the street or in our case estate party. There were quite a few of the old Route Master bus sprayed silver such as the number 49 from Streatham to Shepherd Bush Green, or the number 19 from Tooting Bec to Finsbury Park (now that was a long route). These paraded up and down Bridge Road, just like the wonderful days of old with the Easter parade in Battersea Park (which because of council cuts was stopped) with the fabulous jersey float and a setting of 100,000 blooms. Post boxes were painted silver and the whole country was going to have the biggest party since VE (Victory in Europe).

Everyone gave and made what they can. This was the first time I had eaten chicken, rice and peas, along with a little curried goat. The salt fish and ackee I gave a miss, as at that age I didn't have a cultured palate. Jollof rice and barbecue chicken was delightful fare, along with the standardized egg mayonnaise. There was ham and pickle, cheese and pickle sandwiches, cheese and pineapple, along with cocktail sausages on sticks. For drink we had mixes with every fruit cordial, R whites lemonade, tizer, happy shopper cola for the minors. The grown-ups were awash with Watneys party seven, babycham, blue nun and Captain Morgan rum. The musical sounds covered disco, pop and reggae ringing out all over the Surrey Lane, a togetherness encircled by all. I can still picture Aunty cuddling her newborn great nephew like her life depended on it.

With the words of the recently created school song echoing in my mind (written by Mr. Guy at Bolingbroke primary school), *'we work and we play, learning to live together each day'*, my application for my first choice of secondary school, Battersea County comprehensive school Dagnall Street, was successful. This was the same place of education as my Mum had attended many years earlier when it was located in the old Chesterton building Battersea Park Road. Mum left with a large number of top grade qualifications and now it was my sisters turn entering the 6th form, with babe in arms. I went with Mum to the interview with the head of Tower House and was painted a picture of *'we are going to teach you to remember to get a job'*. But, at least the head of house focused some of the meeting on my sporting ability, especially football. It was sport and creative lessons that really got me through the everyday drudgery of 5-year year torture. If not it would be off into my own imagination as my sanctuary. Our first mission for my new institutionalised educational cycle was go to Waterman's school clothes outfitters Northcote Road SW11, or the Northcote by locals. Since the bugaboo yummy mummy *'shall we meet for a Frappuccino after Christabelle's mindfulness class'* contingent arrived, areas and places have been renamed by upmarket estate agent; between the commons, toast rack, or nappy valley as some called the area! All I needed was a blazer, embossed with the school badge and a tower house school tie, which was duly purchased. None of my really close friends from my primary education were going to the same secondary school, so in my mind it was new friends and relationships to be fashioned. However, the saving grace was that I would have friends who I played football with me in my youth club team and a bond had already been cemented.

The first day of new school was upon me. I set off, shanks' pony style and met one of my friends from our estate who was joining from another school. We were placed in the same tutor group called 1T2. Right away he helped me get rid of my grammar school style tied tie and then showed how his elder brother had demonstrated the working class, estate kid interpretation of the big Winchester knot with a little piece of the end of the cloth protruding out. So now I was in full battle garments for my journey into the abysmal comprehensive academic system; or at least from my experience it was. Our tutor group teacher was one of the old Victorian corporal punishment brigade which at Battersea cowshed a few teachers still possessed. My Sister had the same teacher for maths and the whisper around every pupil he taught was that he was homosexual. This was not a judgement though at this age I can say that I had little understanding. There was still so much ignorance over this. Going back to the 1950/60s a distance family member was gay and so were two close family friends. One of them bit a less than pleasant person's nose in a fight and the other, many years later when my Mum was a manager in a day centre, would come free of charge to perform musical shows to the elderly. He was dressed in the most beautiful women's clothing, actually looked better than some of the female gender. Quantum leaping in my future a little when I was about 17 or 18 entering my first hostelry in Battersea what is described as a crossdresser, a person who dresses in clothes normally only associated with opposite gender, meet, Stella the fella. Sid the mechanic by day, Stella the fella by night, frequented the public bar, and what a delightful and wonderful soul to talk with. I felt loved by Stella as a great friend of my cousin George and as a result threw a protective poncho around me. Many times I witnessed Stella being ridiculed by some 'Brahms and Liszt' individual before pulling a hem of the rah-rah skirt up, asking me to hold the handbag then Stella proceeded to knock the homo neanderthalensis individual spark out; with imaginary birds just like the cartoons tweeting round their head; poleaxed on the public house sawdust floor. There will be more tales! To me if someone loves someone then gender or sexuality should not come into the equation. There should never be any sort of judgement on that person's love for another human being. Love is love and who you fancy, you fancy, it should be no one's opinion who should love, their choice, their life, their love.

Chapter Eight

Artistic Football – A Man with a Plan

Football as a sporting pastime made my adolescence years tremendously pleasurable. I played in goal for the under 11's and our first season was 1976/77 at Caius House Youth Club, Holman Road, in the ACYC league (all combined youth clubs), under the brilliant leadership and management of George Stanley Ennor. He was, without doubt, a man with an unbelievable vision of how football should be played. George based his philosophy on two fundamental principles; fitness and the Dutch way of playing total football.

The first hurdle at Caius, was trying to get past Molly who was a youth leader who had dedicated decades of her life to the well-being of the many children of Battersea. However, woe betide if you try to evade paying you five pence subs! Molly stood guard at the refreshment counter of the small hall by the pool and table tennis table, waiting for everyone to enter Caius. Her tone of voice was at the frequency only the younger generation could hear (probably above 17,000 Hz). Eventually we would succumb and dues would be paid. I still have flashbacks of Molly screaming *'Subs, subs where are your sub'?* Molly had a heart of gold and we all felt the unconditional love she had for the kids. Molly also lived on the Surrey Lane and right up to her passing, which was not that many years back, was a lifelong Chelsea fanatic and season ticket holder. She a true Battersea girl at heart and they just don't make them like Molly any more.

We had two training nights, Mondays and Fridays and where the start of the week was for fitness. With my figure at that time not conducive for prolonged sessions of intensive running training, it was bloody hard work. Somehow though I always found the will to complete what George asked. We would have run through brick walls for George, because he believed in us, and we believed in him. We'd start at 7pm sharp on the long fitness run with exercises on route every Monday throughout the football season. There were about 14 members of our squad, we would line up in two's, akin to soldiers going on a military training run. Our starting point would be Caius, a steady jog at a comfortable pace out onto Lombard Road, turn right near to Westland heliport and past the Raven Inn (which is now a listed building and upmarket restaurant and where originally part of Battersea Village). Its past had tales of smugglers, tunnels to the Thames and it is alleged that Dick Turpin was a visitor (which would ring true with the shenanigans going on at Battersea Common Fields). This was the folklore of Battersea's people past and present and one of our teammate's Dad was the landlord at that time. It was then onto Westbridge Road and past the Surrey Lane Estate.

George is with us, inspiring and motivating (and no I'm not out of breath yet!) then onto the crossroads of Battersea Bridge Road and Parkgate Road. Then we are at the Battersea Park gates entrance at Albert Bridge which was built by Rowland Mason Ordish in 1873, then improved by Sir Joseph Bazalgette. The bridge had the nickname 'the trembling lady' because of its tendency to vibrate. A sign on the original tollbooths, back when you had to pay to cross the bridge, had the words "ALBERT BRIDGE NOTICE, ALL TROOPS MUST BREAK STEP WHEN MARCHING OVER THIS BRIDGE". Chelsea barracks was close by so it made sense. Next, we'd pass the Prince Albert pub, where Prince William in the present day favours the occasional fizzy beer. He is only about a mile from a watering hole where he could go on Battersea Bridge Road, by the Latchmere, and get a light and bitter for the Duke of Cambridge at the Duke of Cambridge! I sound like a London black taxi driver doing the knowledge (licensed cab driver training modules, road and street learning, etc.) or a London tour guide. Then it is into Battersea Park, past the sign by the park keeper's house (where the Duke of Wellington and Earl of Winchilsea had a duel on the 21st March 1829). Battersea Common Fields was a popular spot for dueling so nothing has changed there then! By now we are running parallel with old father Thames on our left hand side. Between us there is a feeling of togetherness and unity, we are at a steady pace and I still have not given up moaning, sulking or walking because I would be letting down George and my teammates. We are running up carriage side north onto the parade, which is the named roads on the perimeter of the park, past the old entrance to the funfair, under the old tree walk and a food kiosk. When I was younger we were served a drink called a snowball; a drink with crushed ice which was the older version of a slush puppy. The children's zoo also in the vicinity the surrounding area by the fair. We passed where the tree walk use to be before moving on to the then old English garden that at this time had a big goldfish in a rectangular shaped pond. Battersea Park was also where the first exhibition football game played under the then recently formed FA (football association) on the 9th January 1864. The park is also listed on the register of historic parks and gardens. Now as we are heading towards the Chelsea Bridge Gate, George has us doing shuttle runs, where the two at the back sprint to the front of the line. I'm alright over ten yards and eighteen yard sprints I am lethal; this being the area of the penalty box. So not a need for an iron lung yet! Then George starts giving us comma+space-ends, left, which means touch the ground with left hand while you're still running, poetry in motion, with me akin to a manatee in the Florida Glades. I'm not giving up as George shouts *'heads'* which means you pretend you're heading an imaginary ball (for me it is catching an imaginary ball). We're then out of the Chelsea Bridge Gate which is opposite the famous Chelsea pie stall (the original stall is now, I believe, in a museum as part of our social history). This gate entrance is where the Chelsea cruise moved from the Kings Road. This is where souped up custom cars come one Saturday every month. Now we are running over Chelsea Bridge and along the embankment as we come to the dreaded shuttle training at Albert Bridge steps. This meant running up and down the steps leading off the bridge. Now this exercise was a killer, and my legs feel like lead; feel that I am running in hobnail boots but my lungs are still full of courage and determination. Right now, I embrace that we are on the stretch back home to our base, Caius House Holman Road. I'm still with my team as we go back over Battersea Bridge and turn left onto Battersea Church Street past all the industrial factories (where now are built million pound studio apartments). We go by St Mary's Church where my Sister had her first marriage in 1980 (but I didn't witness the ceremony because I was outside with my three year old nephew who was playing up and so Uncle Dodger had to be Uncle Dodger!). Back down Lombard Road onto Gwynne Road and left into Yelverton Road. Here there were still terraced houses, though in the process of being demolished as part of the slum clearance. Entombed in corrugated sheets this places would be worth a fortune now. George shouting to us to sprint the last hundred yards and off my little wibble wobble body but I won't fall down. Giving it all I've got because I don't want to let George or my teammates down. As we finish we go straight to the refreshment bar to drink two full pints of water infused orange cordial. I get indigestion and wind because I've gulped the drinks down too fast! Oh do I hanker for those days of yesteryear? Maybe.

Chapter Nine

The Collective Heart of the People

A council estate is a building complex containing a number of council properties and other amenities like schools and shops. The Housing act of 1919 ran right up to the 1980's and was established for the regeneration process for the working class to escape their slum dwellings or low level grade houses and to have a better standard of living accommodation; a token gesture to keep the natives happy and futile in the end? From my experiences I will attempt, for you the reader, a drone view observation into the character and soul of my neck of the woods. In the 1970's, 80's and 90's the Surrey Lane estate was labeled rough, tough and notorious just like most of the Battersea area. Whenever mentioned by others from outside the typical stereotype, based on limited information and media/news coverage, was trotted out. This corresponded to a narrow minded, prejudiced and discriminatory judgement of estate dwellers. So little had changed, and us not losing our charm, from the Battersea Common Fields days where our forebears were called bloody costermongers, vagabonds, waifs and strays. In the present day because materialism has turned Battersea into a place no former area residents can afford to live. I'm not the voice for all in Battersea but the feeling I get from friends when I'm back on the manor is that they wished that they had moved when offered the chance. One friend who still lives in the area told me painfully that ninety percent of his monthly income goes on private rent just so he could be close to his family. This is his support network because he suffers with bouts of clinical depression but he also craves the independence that having his own place brings. I'm told certain estates are resembling ghost towns at weekends as the new residents go back to their parents country abodes. The majority of properties are privately own and are not there for the good of the community. From Battersea you can go by public transport absolutely anywhere, with the Lane now being a desirable district with its 'attractive apartments'; wiping out the maisonettes prefix as the former sounds more gentrified and upmarket (or up your own arse). They have to disassociate from its working class identity to justify rent at two thousand six hundred pound a month and properties going for nye on half a million pound on the Surrey Lane. As my Dad said a while back whilst visiting his old stomping grounds *"Take me back to Bognor boy, Battersea don't feel like home no more"*. Seventy years my Dad lived a true Battersea life but now has no emotional or sentimental connection with the area any more. Answers on a postcard to:

The Bringers of a False Dawn (superficial non community),

A Knob,

170 Battersea Village Bridge Thoroughfare,

Apartment 26 at the Court of Sancroft,

Battersea,

South Chelsea,

South west of London in the Area 11,

Three Artificial Urban Renewal.

One of my abiding memories of growing up is that there were always children out playing. We had to make our own entertainment back then as we didn't have the luxuries and technologies of today's generation. Can it be said that near complete is the takeover of the young with gadgets like X-boxes, PlayStations and computers? Then with social media like Facebook, twitter, instagram, whatsapp etc. the world is at their fingertips but they don't go out to play. I've just worked out what Bluetooth does! The youth of today would be at a loss without their electrical devices as these have become a part of their anatomy. Is there a feeling of emptiness without? I use the electronic world as a tool not out of necessity. If the direction of society is 'likes', 'loves' and 'shares', strike me down with a feather are we heading for a troublesome future. As humans, we need human interaction and connection and this is fundamental to our existence. When we played out, we played out; and let us be clear we would have got on our parents nerves if we had stayed in all the time.

As we were enterprising Kids we made our own entertainment in the many forms of enjoyment, and this included visits to Battersea Park adventure playground, known locally as The Jungle. The health and safety executive would have had kittens if they had witnessed the ropes, swings and apparatus in operation. Unthoughtful to the danger to us kids with the peril of our body parts in constant jeopardy, but we didn't care with our cavalier approach to life. Usually in school holidays and after school, a group of us would meet down in the small red square, then decide it was a trip to the jungle for the days pleasure. Into Four Buoys, the estate newsagent sweet shop, to stock up on calories for this work out day spent at The Jungle. With such goodies as the lucky bags, Smiths savoury vinegar crisps (no longer made though similar to today's pickled onion flavor), a couple of cans of top deck shandy for hydration and a Texan chewy chocolate bar for energy; and all of those with fifty pence! This was given by your parents for the day just to get rid of you. Maybe, just maybe, if you rationed your daily pocket money wisely there would be a chance that you were in good order with the funds after your day of play for a ninety nine from Mr. whippy, or a cider lolly from the Bedford CF ice cream van stationed by the paddling pool. Such carefree days.

There was usually three to five of us from the concrete jungle of The Surrey Lane for our short journey to the jungle by the small gate entrance on Albert Bridge Road. Into the park and past where my Dad said during WW2 there were allotments helping the war effort. Then the one o/clock club was in view, a sort of kindergarten, playgroup where anyone or any child under five or preschool could attend without extortionate fees. This was a time to give parents a little respite in a non-judgmental environment where the little people could play safely. To get to The Jungle you had to go through the children's playground, swings, slides etc., but if you wanted a more thrill seeking act in this arena of daredevil style play, a jaunt up to what was named the American swings at Queens Circus Gate at Chelsea Bridge Road. Here your amusement came on such equipment as the 'witches' hat' or the 'makers name', the 'conical wave' (a conical swing balanced on a central pole which oscillated unpredictably and invented by Charles Wicksteed for his park in Kettering Northamptonshire). Or even the swing boat which was manually operated by weight distribution of aforementioned two children with a motion when standing up. Akin to a normal swing but instead of sitting down standing up, you were getting a workout and didn't even know it.

The Jungle got its defining name through the biggest rope 'The Tarzan Swing' which was an absolutely massive rope looped through an enormous oak tree. The fastening procedure meant just holding the rope and wrapping your legs around the giant knot at its end; this was your only safety harness! With two landing stages at either side of the rope's swing limits of the extension, boarding was a must and a test of strength and dynamic tension capabilities of the first foolhardy soul on the rope.

Once one was aboard the objective was to get as many fearless individuals onto the rope. Many times I've witnessed and experienced countless youngsters either dropping off resembling a ripe apple (proving Newton's law of gravity). Alternatively, rope burns with blisters on hands comparable to a navy digging tunnels from twelve-hour shift with a pickaxe. A short limp to the guardians of the Jungle in their basic hut (with one table tennis table and the whiff of paint as there was always a creative art group in progress) and in their possession we were fortunate that they had a first aid kit. Importantly, this always consisted of bandages, germolene, plaster and TCP and there was always a whiff of TCP in the Jungle air space with its injured Johnny Weissmuller's (the inspiration for our Jungle shenanigans).

There was a very early evolutionary zip-line (aerial runway), which consisted of a pulley suspended on cable. Here we launched ourselves off a landing platform around twenty feet high and hung on for dear life to just a rope loop attached to the pulley wheel fixed onto the wire. We proceeded to descend at a rate of knots again without any safety device tethering us to the line in case we lost our grip, with gravity, motion and weight accelerating our speed. The end to our journey of freedom came with the ride abruptly coming to stop by a large break knot at the end of the wire. Our weighted body mass catapulted us into a reverse with half spin double pike dismount, only to land on a thin layer of wood chippings and then getting up stinking of creosote as the chips were soaked in the stuff.

The totem pole swing of fright was another rope based structure which today would not only be banned it would never have been constructed in the first place. It was a very basic contraption where you put your hands again on a loop on a rope attached to the top of a telegraph pole. The banks were cut away, so in a running and swinging circumference movement you left one bank and returned on the other after completing one hundred and eighty degrees; this was mathematics on the go! Finally, we had the wooden slatted bog standard go kart track which ran right through the centre of the Jungle. Whilst there were no Lewis Hamilton's or Juan (John)Manuel Fangio born in The Jungle, James Hunt did live at 220 Battersea Bridge Road in the mid 1970's. I remember vividly as a minor, Mr. Hunt bare footed on a Sunday morning collecting his papers from the estate shops.

Our karts were made out of scaffold boards and planks of untreated wood (many a splinter up your Harris!) with a steering mechanism of a piece of rope attached to the front axle for a bit left and a bit right control. Again, I had witnessed many youth of yesterday not doing their green cross code by failing to look right, look left, and look right again! In the instances where they didn't look right, didn't look left, and didn't look right again they came a cropper. The driver of the kart and track turned into the film set of Death Race 2000 where the totalitarian regime in a dystopian society was the transcontinental road to knock the unaware over and receive points. The jungle kart track became bystander to many mortal souls knocked over arsehole to breakfast time, but no points were gained! The reliable TPC magic solution administered by the jungle elders always, but always, made everything right.

The beating heart of The Jungle was the children from the surrounding estates. Within walking distance to the park came school friends and youth club friends. I was always there with my cousin Tony just enjoying our time in the adventure playground; The Jungle being our inner city entertainment, our Disneyland, our evolution of character and personality through direct experience. This was within reach of the working people before the corporate business take over that now means the entrance fee is a considerable sum of money!

Chapter Ten

A Pupil of Indifference or a Unique Thinker?

My imagination has always been my software for working out what I don't understand. I realised, confirmed by neuroscience, that I have always been a right sided thinking individual. This represents the creative, imaginative, general, intuitive, conceptual, big picture, heuristic, empathetic, figurative and the irregular (in contrast to the sided emphasis on the analytical, logical, precise, repetitive, organised, details, scientific, detached, literal and sequential). I have had, even from a very tender age, the capacity to have a creative and abstract observation of life. 1T2 my tutor group class (abbreviation of one tower two) was roughly thirty two pupils, again a wide spectrum of diverse ethnic backgrounds, which was so natural to me after my six years of upbringing on the Surrey Lane. However, I felt an air of separation already, with racial differences becoming apparent from whom sat next to who. First we were given a dairy for lesson planning and homework, my mind was already thinking *'why homework?'* haven't the teachers got enough time to educate us properly in the school time? Our day was made up of seven periods and we studied a combination of maths, English, physics, French, social studies, religious education, woodwork, metalwork, technical drawing, home economics, music and games/PE. This curriculum hadn't changed much from the Victorian era and was designed for a population where work was essentially factory fodder. The subjects had little relevance to our lives and this was my itinerary for the next three years, can't wait!

The saving grace would be found in some the subjects where there were opportunities to use the creative part of the mind rather than the majority which were just a test of memory. I'm a great believer that school should not teach you what to think but more fundamentally how to think.

My first lesson and period of school-based torment was double maths, where after a multiple-choice exam I was placed in the divvy (thick) group. Later in life, some are lucky to realise that they do have a good understanding of the mathematical processes despite the early label from teachers. In my case the tests, with their one cap fits all mentality, left me in the bottom group. However, the one thing I did remember was Pi; twenty two over seven or three point one four. It is defined as the ratio of a circle's circumference to its diameter, and it has other equivalent definitions. If only the maths could have been combined with a bit of history and told me that Pythagoras of Samos was an ancient Ionian philosopher and that he had useful insights about life, musica universalis, and metempsychosis (transmigration of souls) I would have been so engaged I would have been happy with a whole day of maths! This would have encouraged a zest for learning rather than me sitting there thinking *'I wonder what Mum's cooking for dinner tonight?'*

Another must for us kids from the local estates was a regular foray to the Latchmere Public Baths, which combined public bathing and self-laundry. I was a regular at the Latchmere where I could dive, before I could swim, school swimming lessons from Bolingbroke were taught there, and a venue three generations of our family attended. 'Penny bare bums' was the local nickname acquired way back in time when swimming trunks were a luxury to the local working class. As a result, at the boys pool you could go and have a swim in your birthday suit, as bare as the day you were born. Latchmere also had within its beautiful Victorian building a public baths where you would pay a small fee and have a hot water bath. An attendant who would control the hot and cold water running into your bath looked you after. But beware, the shout *'more cold in number two'* when you got the bath number wrong and you would hear someone you didn't know bellowing *'turn that flipping cold off'*. There was even fun and enjoyment when you visited for your weekly bathing experience. All the terraced houses at this time, occupied by the working class of Battersea, still had outside toilets and a tin bath in the scullery for your hygiene. My Dad said his parents said use to give him a tanner to have a bath at the Latchmere, but he would go swimming in the pool, and still have enough money for a lovely hot chocolate when he'd finished. When arriving home and asked '*you had a bath boy?*' he would reply '*of course I have Mum*'! Every school holiday, summer and winter there was always on the agenda of things to do a visit to the Latchmere Baths. We had our trunks wrapped up in a towel, and a plastic bag to carry them in if you were lucky. Again, you'd meet all your mates for the fifteen minute walk from the Surrey Lane to the Baths, pay your five pence to get into the mixed pool via the men's changing room. We'd go to the counter at the end and get our metal clothes basket, which weighed a tonne and was shaped like a framework of a blazer. It had a cage in bottom for your shoes, the framework for your clothes and most importantly held your wristband (blue, red or green) for when it was your timed period finished in the pool. The pool attendant/lifeguard would blow his or her whistle with the intensity of a referee blowing for kick off in a world cup final, and then scream, *'ALL BLUE BANDS OUT'*. To get back to the changing room you had to go through a shallow dip pool full of disinfectant, just in case you had trench foot or verruca. Then you came into the wonderful atmosphere of the mixed pool, which was a multi-purpose venue and had water polo goals suspended from the pool ceiling. The pool had the facility to be covered with wooden flooring for the benefit of local boxing shows and at the deep end you had a small three fixed stage diving platform, akin to a gold, silver and bronze rostrum. You could smell the chloride in the air and knew that your eyes were going to sting once you had done your Mark Spitz impersonation and time in the pool. I once saved a young lads life who was on a visit from a playscheme from the estate. He decided to jump right into the deep end and sunk down to the bottom. By this I was a swimmer of experience and had spotted what he had done. I dived straight in, pulled him up to the surface coughing and gasping and then got him to the side of the pool. He was then taken by first aider to get checked out. Those lifesaver badges we did in primary school, where we had to doggy paddle in our pajamas and get the big heavy black rubber brick from the deep end, did come in useful after all. Getting changed we would flick our mates with the wet towel like a whip, and then the highlight, as it was with my father was the vending machine with its lava hot drinking chocolate! Alas, that big graceful Victorian building was demolished in the 1980's and replaced with a theme based pool with its vogue (at the time) wave machine. It was renamed The Latchmere Leisure Centre. This change of moniker meant a change of character and personality (you couldn't flick people with your towel anymore!).

Chapter Eleven

An Ode to our Peculiar Colloquialisms

Back in the day when basketball boots were bumper boots, and not just bumpers on a car.

When trainers were plimsolls, before trainers were coaches who tutored you in sport.

And a coach or charabanc was a ride to the coast,

When wicked meant bad, not good.

When sick meant you were ill not stylish or glamorous.

When fat was an oversize, not phat to be great.

When dates were a Christmas treat and good for the bowels and not going out with a girl, lying you were well endowed.

When a tear up meant ripping not having a fight, or to have a ripping body was a wonderful sight.

Someone who is fit was a term of allure to another, not shaking on the floor, friends getting your Mother,

When dope in street talk meant divvy or thick, not a big reefer of smoke or soap bar brick.

When Charlie was just your mates name not a gramme of coke.

When beef was a Sunday meal not a problem with another.

When your Mum dressed you in a vest for your infant years to keep out the chill, you rebelled in growing up and dispensed with the vest.

But now, in middle age the vest makes a comfortable and timely return. It's funny the life cycle of a vest.

Friday night was our other night of training with George at the Battersea Sports Centre, Hope Street SW11. Again, we had to jog from Caius to the Centre which was around half a mile away in order to train, to learn, to teach, to enable us as a team to play the way quality football should be expressed. Right we are not getting away with not running and warming up, so in pairs again, I would go with anyone, usually settled myself in the middle so not to fall behind. Off we go with George leading, a steady pace jogging around the perimeter fence of the closed in football pen. I know this is not going to be a destroyer of my lung capacity like Monday's training night. About ten times around the five aside pitch, left, right, touching the ground, come to a rest. Then stretching was the next exercise, *'stretch those hamstrings Dodger English'* George would shout, big breath in through the nose and out through the mouth, in a swinging pendulum motion with your arms, left hand touches right toe and right hand touches left toe. We still have not been near a ball yet, but once we are loose and ready, the lesson begins.

Firstly, we all had a ball each to dribble and do keepy uppies. George would say the ball is your friend and only full of air, then we would get into groups of two, parallel, facing each other, ten yards apart, passing one touch, two and three scenarios where the ball would always be under our control. I would do all the ball control training with the team and that's why in my later years, when the calling to be a goalkeeper subsided and when I retired from youth football, I saw myself as a bit of a Kerry Dixon Style centre forward. I started playing for Old Grammarians 7th XI (Battersea Grammar School). I was top scorer for the season, including three hat tricks playing against men just near pension age. By then my outer frame had grown considerably, and so my team supplied shirt had to be poured on rather than put on. My shorts were so tight I had the voice of a soprano singer, between the C4 and C6, but I loved every minute.

The first season as Caius under elevens we won the league and cup double at our first attempt; beating in The final at West London Stadium Wormwood Scrubs a team called Wormolt (featuring a young Dennis Wise, playing for the opposition and later becoming a professional at Wimbledon, Chelsea and England). The match report in the local paper quoted, *'If Ron Greenwood wants the blueprint for a brighter England future he would have done no harm by watching these brilliant young football teams, play football the way it should be played!*'. As a team we went on to greater heights which I shall tell in later chapters.

By now, through a complicated route of local government funding we were able to have built a community hall just on a grassed area in front of Gardiner House. This was the other side to the big red square where the classic football matches of twenty a-side were commonplace, at times against other estates. I've scored many a critical injury time winner though in reality it was the first team to twenty. I was a top class goal hanger which in street football terminology is where you stand by the goal waiting for glory (while the energetic and workmanlike team members do all the hard graft). This is the infamous big red square which had three steps leading down into its bowl, where I slipped whilst trying to drop kick a football, landing bang on my coccyx and have suffered with sciatica ever since (and even giving me jip when I am writing this now!).

Much of our time was spent at a playscheme. For those not in the know, this a local project providing recreational facilities and activities for children for certain periods of time, typically during school holidays, and the Surrey Lane estate playscheme was for two weeks within the school six-week holiday period. Nearly every child on the estate from six to sixteen attended the playscheme. We even had one lad join us from another estate, the legendary 'Sugar' Ray Henry (RIP), and he went on to be an inspirational youth leader, a youth mentor who is sadly no longer with us. We had the Wandsworth community social worker with us on the playscheme. The first was John who was a local and was with us for a few years before Mick a Liverpudlian man took over. They attended everyday and even came on our legendary camping trips (a sort of Carry on Camping for under sixteens).

These social workers were brilliant individuals who realised that you had to know the community you were serving; to become one and immerse yourself in the community. They certainly did and were respected by all.

My Mum was one of the playscheme leaders, along with a woman named Ann who everyone called Bod (a shortening of her name 'Bodnar' and also the name of a popular kids TV programme of the time). Many of the estate mum's who had the time would help with all the activities and events we all took part in. The playscheme opening times were 9am till 4pm and you would have kids waiting outside the tenants' hall at 8:30am after their parents had gone to work and sort of chucked them out.

Back then there were quite a few options for funding and grant opportunities, especially if you had the community social worker involved and could witness the good and positive impact it was having on the younger generation of Battersea. There were no estate gangs, no knife crime and no social exclusion. And the conclusion? Positive action by caring and protective adults initiates a beneficial evolution of a generation helping them become more effective adults with a foundation built on worthy principles and values.

Chapter Twelve

Escape from the City

We had a few camping excursion trips together and the first was to a camping site at Foots Cray Bexley Kent. This was a very ordinary place with the vast majority of locals being white working class. Our kids came from more diverse and multicultural backgrounds and we did have an issue when some kids from a local estate were on land near the camp and racially abused our estate youngsters. This was heard by one of the Caucasian older kids, who so happened to have two mixed heritage siblings and, acting out of protection for the child being abused, knocked out the two abusers. Whilst I am not an advocate of violence, they deserved it though his main concern was that he had got blood from one the abusers all over his army green trousers. This young man from the estate later in life chopped off a man's arm after an argument in a pub and served a long prison sentence. As a young person he was beaten by his step- father with a belt and metal dog lead, and I witnessed it. No wonder his head was mucked up in childhood and turned to violence in adulthood. As I always say I never judge anybody. This was not our most successful tenure of a first camping trip. Whilst on a day out to Camber Sands being a greedy sod I brought a massive bag of honeycomb and stuffed the lot in a matter of minutes. As a result I was sick, with projectile vomiting all the way on the journey back to the campsite, whilst the heavens opened up with a gigantic thunderstorm. On arriving back we realised that all of our clothes and sleeping bags were drenched. Our lack of camping knowledge meant we had not put everything into black bin liners to keep dry. That night everyone had to sleep in the catering tent, and let me tell you, the countryside is still cold in the middle of the night (we knew how Scott of the Antarctic felt!). One poor lad had a tummy upset, bad wind and near on touching cloth! Farting Alec was encouraged to sleep outside the tent under the cover of a tree with plentiful branches and leaves for protection.

Our next foray to pastures new was a property owned by Wandsworth Council called Bassett Coach House Monkton Combe near Bath in Somerset (Wiltshire borders). It is now a beautiful hotel and private residence, within foot walking distance of the Kennet and Avon canal and the River Avon. On the morning of our departure, four hired minibuses awaited to be boarded with about thirty kids and around ten helpers, including Mick the Liverpudlian social worker. For our travels west for all of us this was a passage into the undiscovered Somerset wilderness. Some of the estate kids had never ventured out of Battersea or even been on holiday, so there was an atmosphere of excitement as the inner city expedition was a rolling in the

Blue Toyota Hiace minibuses wheels. Out of London and onto the M4 and just one straight road we come to our place of occupation for the next five days and nights. A stop in the services on the M4 for a toilet break and only one break allowed as we have got to jog on as we have only done thirty miles with another seventy-three to do. On arrival at our destination, decamping from the minibuses and proceeding to our plain canvas ridge tents to throw down our backpacks and sundries and make time to explore. The elders on the trip wanted a cup of tea but no one had thought to bring along a fresh pint of milk! But fortunately one of the kids from the estate piped up *'I've got a pint in my backpack!'* This young individual was called Michael but went by the nickname 'Pengie', because Michael had ten to two feet or a Charlie Chaplin gate. When he laughed he sounded the same as Burgess Meredith (a virtuoso American who played the Penguin in the original TV series of Batman which was constantly broadcast on British TV during the 1960's and 70's). I did enter a competition once on the Saturday morning kids show Tiswas (this is Saturday, what a Saturday) when Adam West, the original Batman, was appearing and you had to count all the Batman lyrics in the theme tune, but to my sorrow I did not win. There must have been at least thirty children from the estate on our adventure, akin to the united nations on tour, we were so lucky to have the River Avon just a short walk through the woods. Next to the river was the Kennet and Avon canal which at that time was dry in most places. It was located across the main Wessex main line bath to Westbury railway and the Dundas Aqueduct. The latter is made of beautiful bath stone, designed by John Rennie and constructed in 1801. The aqueduct carried the Kennet and Avon Canal over the River Avon and there is an area adjacent called Brassknocker Basin. Down the side of the aqueduct through a very steep gradient wooded area and there for us to us to use was a jetty for the 'piscatorians' (fisherperson). There was also a canoe house with instructors, so we could go up and down the River Avon at our hearts content. This was a bit different from the River Thames at the time with its heavy industrial landscape and factories all along its banks. With smoke billowing from chimneys just like when the genius poet William Blake wrote Jerusalem with the words 'dark and satanic mills', a symbolic reference to a factory that was burnt down near his home in Peckham. Blake realised that the true God (a goodness of orderly direction) was the human imagination. This is a feeling that connects with me deeply.

We had such joyous times on those trips, not washing for five days, just brushing our teeth. We went to bed in all our clothes, just taking our shoes off, waking up feeling like we've slept on a concrete slab all night. Adults and kids alike sitting around the campfire burning our toast and marshmallows, talking about our hopes and dreams for the future; what wonderful unruffled days!

The three years of compulsory state lessons didn't mean that it was all hard work and toil, for there were classes offering an opportunity for my creative expression. I wanted to be allowed to develop and thrive, although at this time of my life I really did not understand how my creative and unique thinking processes were different to everyone else.

One compulsory schooling class I just did not get was French! Firstly we had to have a French name and you would think it would be the French interpretation of Stephen. But no, our French teacher decided I should be called Didier, which in French means Derek. so now I'm Derek English which I didn't mind in the classroom but the teacher insisted on calling me it every time that she saw me about the school thinking I would become a great French linguist. In reality after three years of French studies all I can remember is the president at that time was Valery Giscard d'Estaing, La Gare means the train station, (handy if I was working for Eurostar) and Les Boulangerie which is a French bakers shop. Now don't get me wrong I would love to have learnt a language. However, it wasn't really made relevant to a working class kid from a council estate. Those who wrote the curriculum should have wised up to that, if there was any chance of us developing a taste for languages. As you can see from these chronicles, I love language!

Unfortunately, instead of being inspired to learn a language I was known after a certain infamy in French. One really hot summer's day I returned from lunch after going home for my dinner. I consumed a strawberry yogurt and after having one of my funny turns (sick headache), I began to honk my guts up in the French lesson. A strawberry pink fusion went all over my old wooden school desk and filled the ink pot which was no longer in use (that's how old the school furniture was). Finally it went all down myself though fortunately avoided my classmate at the adjoining desk. I got sent home straight away. Luckily Mum was not in she was out working doing her cleaning job. I got home just in time to watch Crown Court on ITV with its haunting theme tune, then over to the BBC to watch the afternoon play.

Games were always enjoyable because of my natural ability as a goalkeeper. I represented the school team every Saturday morning at Morden Sports Field, Morden Park, where my natural ability for golf was cultured playing the pitch and putt par three with my Grandfather Tom English from a very early age.

Drama was another enjoyable lesson as we would go to local theatres and watch plays by Shakespeare including Macbeth (the Scottish play for the thespians out there!). I remember being enchanted by the rhythm of prose and dialogue of Shakespeare's masterpieces. In particular the lines taken from Hamlet, *'This above all, to thine own self be true, and it must follow, as the night the day, thou canst not then be false to any man'* have helped me through the years and hopefully made me wiser. I have always observed drama from a directors and writer's viewpoint but really have not got a clue why?

Home economics was split between cooking and needlework. Cooking was a pleasant time because we always ate what we cooked. For needlework I liked creating something out of nothing and I did so happen to make a rather good pillow in the shape of an owl, which I believe is still up in our loft.

Woodwork, metalwork and technical drawing were again creative subjects so my boredom never set in. One distinct memory in woodwork resulted in a 'coming together' of two pupils. One pupil proceeded to 'lump' the other as he had been abused racially. He took a wooden mallet which he ended up striking the other with. The result, whilst not funny, did look like a scene from a Hanna and Barbera cartoon!

Art I really loved especially pottery where once we were given the task of creating anything we wanted and I produced a clay Frankenstein's monster. It was about twelve inches high with a great big penis, thinking that I would get in trouble by my Art teacher. Instead, to my surprise, I was congratulated on my artistic expression and given double 'A' in Art for my term report. In the same class one of the pupils had, over a period of time, changed his identity into a skinhead (possibly motivated by a desire to fit in). It was a shame that he was attracted to such extremist ideology on race. He was drawing swastikas in his drawing pad, the teacher went to get the deputy head, on returning with the senior teacher was asked *'what the bloody hell are you doing boy?'*. The pupil replied, *'I want to be a Nazi Sir'*, the Deputy Head called his bluff by saying *'ok then, you can come and sit outside my office and draw a thousand of these'*, now that's a new interpretation of doing lines! Racism was a daily occurrence for our minority ethnic groups back when I was growing up and this is part of the narrative in my storytelling. It was horrible to encounter and always upset me. Back then I had been asked many times why I had black friends. To avoid confrontation I would usually reply *'they are just my friends'*! It was very difficult to understand what lay behind this as a teenager. I am aware now of the debate around 'colour blindness' and I realise that my friends were black and that I didn't need to make any excuses. I did see colour and was certainly aware that my black friends were often treated differently. But I maintain that at the heart of our friendship colour was not the defining factor. Once on my birthday I was kissed by a beautiful girl named Patricia. She was black and was a year older than me in school. I knew her from the Surrey Lane, the racist element of my classmates ridiculed me, but I did not give a damn. This probably accounts for my attitude of being very around friendships. I bumped into one of these 'racist minds' that went to my school. It was in The Blue Orchid nightclub Croydon in 1995. At school, he used to read the National Front Newspaper in the classroom. Guess what? He had not changed!

RE (religious education) was not everyone's favourite lesson but one that really made me think. We had the school's headteacher for this lesson, and for some strange reason I got on very well with him. He said that I had a good foundation of principles, morals and values even at this young age (God knows what he was on about but he did encourage me to take RE as a choice in my final two years). If my path was different I could have been the Revd. Canon Stephen English; but I was never destined to go that way. Finally, I have to mention Music which was compulsory for the first three years. We ended up playing all sorts of simple instruments like the triangle and the glockenspiel. We would accompany songs like 'Yellow Bird' (the original title was 'Choucoune' a nineteenth century Haitian Creole song composed by Michael Mauleart Monton with lyrics from Oswald Durand's poem). This praises the beauty of Haitian women of that nickname, and a beautiful version of Yellow Bird is sung by the The Mills Brothers. Another song was 'Guantanamera' written by Jose Marti and Julian Orbon in an afro-Cuban jazz style. The original interpretation had a romantic spin and a love affair gone awry, it was the story of a woman who gets fed up and leaves the man after being mistreated, possibly by his infidelity. When you search a little you discover the deeper meaning.

I was given an opportunity to put my name on a list to have drumming lessons, which meant that I would get out one of my boring subjects called ESS (English and Social Studies combined). There was limited content and taught by a teacher who had a canny resemblance to Marc Bolan of T-Rex. Likewise, there was little to commend Math's with a little rotund teacher of five foot tall who had a very short temper and an urge to throw chalkboard cleaners and his big bunch of keys at pupils. He once threw them at the wrong individual who propelled the keys in the return direction whilst shouting, *'here's your keys back fatty'*, and *'you know what you can do with math's?'* and just walked out of the class. I was chosen, along with a mate from my tutor group whom I played football with. It was two lessons a week of forty minutes, what a touch! Off I go up to Readings Record Store Clapham Junction in the quest for my own drumsticks. Fortunately, they had many types including wooden tips and nylon tips for the more advanced percussionist. I started with the basic sticks (don't bang too hard before you understand the rhythm and timing). I really loved drumming and got to quite a good standard and even got a very small part playing the cabasa in the school band (a cabasa is like the maracas but instead of a wide cylinder wrapped around with a steel ball chain). Looking back, music was another subject I wished I had opted for (my

Dad was a drummer in skiffle bands so I had some sort of timing and rhythmical intent).

Corporal punishment was still prevalent while I was attending secondary school; the slipper and cane being the weapons of choice. My tutor group teacher was a bit handy with the slipper (was it his fetish for hitting boys that floated his boat?). I encountered this out of date punishment only on one occasion and yes the slipper did hurt! We also had an English teacher who was inclined to brutality with his cane beside him on his desk. I received the cane from him for talking in class, a very petty crime and this was an over the top punishment. Again this teacher got his karmic due as, whilst caning one of my classmates so hard he ended up splitting and cutting the cheeks of the pupils arse so bad the boy could not sit down. The lad told his parents and his father came to the school and attacked the abusing teacher in our English lesson. Senior staff were called and the police got involved; both these teachers were eventually retired off and these incidents were brushed under the carpet (that's how it was back then). A few years later I did so happen to see my brutal English teacher whilst fishing with my cousin George at Hampton Court. The said teacher was walking past us; I told my cousin who wanted to throw him in the River Thames! However, I told him to leave it as what he did would be on his conscience. I said *'Hello Sir how are you?'*, he recognised me as well with a quite pleasant response. He informed me that he had an incurable disease; the universe pays back in mysterious ways. In that moment I forgave him.

Chapter Thirteen

Death is not the Opposite of Life

Where there is life there is death, and when there is death, there must become life!

I truly understand Death is not an easy subject to talk about especially for me after losing my Mum recently. This is an inner anguish and sorrow and the realisation you are never going to be able see that person ever again. You have to have, within you, an 'accepted loss' rather than pretend it's not happening. The love you have for your Mother, Father, Grandparents etc., never dies. One fundamental thing we should all comprehend about our existence is that we are all going to die one day; no gets out of life alive. There is birth and there is death! So please endeavour to live life to the fall and in the moment, if you have a roof over your head, a bed to sleep on, food to eat and love from family and friends you are rich and should feel blessed.

My Grandfather, George James (born 1906 died 1971) was a true Battersea man but died just six months after over fifty years of work. Back then you left school at thirteen and he never got time to enjoy his retirement with my Nan Lizzy 'don't mess about with me' James. He didn't get the chance to spend time with his daughters who he absolutely adored; Betty, Eileen (my Mum) and Maureen. Neither did he witness his Grandchildren growing up into good human beings. I was only five at the time at the death of this close family member and, whilst I saw the emotional pain that everyone was suffering, at that age I had no deep comprehension of this feeling.

The Surrey Lane community was in collective mourning. This was especially so when the death is of a younger person and totally unexpected. There were two circumstances of untimely deaths which both affected West Indian families from the estate. The first was of a young man, a very talented footballer, who was killed in a car crash in the small hours on a summer Sunday morning. He was returning from a 'blues party' with three others in a vehicle on a section of road just walking distance from the estate. I remember being told of his passing on the Sunday morning and going up to the scene of the incident and just looking at the lamppost they had careered into. I was filled with disbelief and utter shock. This young man was not an original estate resident, as he arrived after the Surrey Lane had been going for a few years, but the shock came from the fact that I had been talking to him only three days earlier. Even back then, with little maturity, it gave me a sense of the fragility of life; one moment we are here, and if fate plays its way, the next you are gone!

The other sombre time involved one of our balcony neighbours, who had a daughter who sadly passed away far too early. This young lady had just had a baby daughter and was full of life for her newborn. I can remember this day vividly, it was a Wednesday evening and Mum, Dad and I were sitting in the living room watching television. It was getting quite late and there was knock on the door. I got up to answer it, and it was a neighbour from a few doors away in absolute floods of tears and pain etch all over her face. She said *'Steve, Steve is your Mum there?'* I replied 'of course'. I called Mum to the door and went back into the front room thinking there is something badly wrong here. Mum went to the door and then the lady started shouting, *'she's gone Eileen, she's died Eileen, they could not wake her up Eileen'.* My Mum calmly took our neighbour into her arms, and comforted her like my Mums life depended on it. Mum took the distressed women into the kitchen and shut the door. I could hear from the front room the most horrendous primal scream I have ever heard in my life. It was two mothers entwined by the heart felt unconditional love for their children coming together; one supporting the other in the darkest time of her life. A parent losing a child must be the most immense torture with emotional turmoil a Mother can ever experience. She gave birth to the child, her DNA was the same, and now the child was gone! My Mum comforted the lady until the early hours until other family members arrived and then we went to bed.

It taught me that in life that you have to have an inner will and strength when you don't feel like carrying on. Always give gratitude that you wake up in the morning, millions don't! Be nice, and if you don't like someone don't hate them. As my Mum always told me hate is such a horrible word. If someone wrongs you forgive them because then you hold the power and it's no good waiting to take revenge because it only creates negative emotions. Experiences, situations and life itself challenges all of us but it is what we learn that makes us a better human beings.

George our coach and manager was not one to become complacent with our football squad. Players left and new players came in. When we finally finished our youth football career at under sixteen, I truly believe that no other team in the UK at our age group would have beaten us. I still have a trophy cabinet at home full of medals won playing football. I say this not out of pride or ego, but just how bloody hard my teammates and I worked our arses off to reach that standard (an unconscious reminder that if you work hard and are smart in life you can achieve anything you want). When we were U14s, we played a team from Peterborough in a friendly game at Wandsworth Common. We were representing the ACYC league and they were supposedly the best team representing the Peterborough Youth League system. I think we beat them nineteen nil and I always remember Peterborough's manager shouting at the left back because our forward was running past him like he was standing still. The dialogue went something like, *'why don't you tackle him'* and the left back shouted the reply *'tackle him! I can't even bloody catch him. He is like Pele'*. And that is how good our team was. There was always some intense rivalry especially with a team called Wandsworth Parks. The games were always a battle on the park with one infamous game when we beat them at Wandsworth Common. Our manager George got into a confrontation with their manager. To George we were his boys, and he would protect us to the end. Their manager got a bit lippy, and you knew when George was about to explode because he would use the word 'Pal'. This meant trouble and it became a stand off in middle of the pitch between George and their manager. Someone had a pushbike, have not got a clue whose it was, but George was in the process of putting the bike over the opposing managers head like a hoopla ring trying to win a goldfish at Battersea funfair. Somehow hot chocolate drink got disposed over their manager's head (George's wife use to make flasks of hot drinks for half time in the freezing winter games). No one witnessed who had done it but luckily it was a few hours old and not piping hot! That was our mentality as a team and reflected a collective desire to win; a tribal instinct that we were all in it together whatever the outcome or result. As I've said before I don't advocate violence but that's the deep meaning and connection we had with the manager and his lads.

I am back in touch with a few teammates from our youth football days and we have had totally different life paths, especially me. However, we seem to have emerged once more into each other's lives and these friends were my encouragement to tell my story. Even in summer months we had little time off from our tough training schedules. After about two weeks into the six week break we were back into pre-season training on those summer Sunday mornings at Battersea park (just by the bowling green sweating our guts out for glory). That was the difference between us and other teams, we were relentless in our pursuit of progression. This was not just about footballing ability but our attitude, character and personality as young lads. We may have been youth football (which was amateur by default) but we definitely had a professional mindset. We did lose on the odd occasion though this was due to us 'not turning up' as a team or playing to the best of our ability. But that was a positive thing because there was always room for us to improve. We won the league and cup double four years on the trot and won the Inter London League trophy with the ACYC team made mostly of players from our team. George also managed the ACYC team and just wanted us to represent the league but this was not allowed by the league chairman. As a result, we had to have lads from other teams and one player from one of the teams signed for us the next season. We played in the London cup semi-final and got beaten three two by a team from south east London who were far better than us on the day. Eventually our manager decided we needed better competition and opponents every game so after our under fourteen season finished we not only changed leagues we moved club and went from Caius to Devas Youth Club Stormont Road. Here we had much better training facilities and the league we were entering a much bigger catchment area of teams (The Shirley and District under fifteens). The result meant that we had harder games each week against the best players from the south London area. The majority of these players were in teams already involved in what are now called academies at professional clubs. This development was a new and exciting adventure for all of us.

Chapter Fourteen

Chosen Subjects?

After three years of mandatory schooling it was time for me to choose my subjects for my final two years of totalitarian education. The lessons, on reflection, did little to prepare us for the trials and tribulations of real life. Reflection and contemplation are great tools for inner growth. Every parents evening my folks were told that it was up to me if I wanted to learn; learn what? Algebra? I didn't understand algebra because nobody shared its mysteries. English and Social studies, the English part of learning was OK, but the social studies part was crap, a dogmatic teaching based on Britain's imperialistic history with hardly any mention of other cultures. Battersea had John Richard Archer a black politician and in 1913 was elected as the Mayor of Battersea, becoming the first black Mayor in London. In 2004 he was chosen for the hundred great black Britons list. He was part of our identity in Battersea and half our class was black. It is beyond comprehension to me and when I questioned the teacher on whether there could be a bit more breath to our lessons he replied *'if you don't want to learn that is up to you. I have thirty other kids in this class and you are the minority, if you want a dead end job then don't learn'.* learn what? That King Henry VIII had loads of wives and when he failed to secure an annulment to Catherine of Aragon in 1534 he thought I know what, I will start my own church! I'll have my own Church of England so I can behead as many wives as I want, because I am the ruler and I am in charge and all my subjects will do as I say. Is this the menu that we were supposed to believe in as a good education? Sir Ken Robinson speaks in a most articulate manner on this topic and highlights that the young no longer believe that merely attending school will result in a fulfilling career. I would urge all parents to listen to what he has to say and make up your own mind!

The work that I enjoy I will put my all into whereas work that is meaningless, and merely for the purpose of existing (paying the bills, etc.), I have trouble committing to. From a young age I have always been surrounded by older individuals and perhaps they have subconsciously imparted an abundance of wisdom. One of my first paid jobs was with my Grandfather Tom English who raced his greyhounds at Aldershot stock car track at Tongham. This also incorporated on the perimetre a greyhound flapping track which is an unlicensed greyhound track not covered by the rules and regulations of the GRA (Greyhound Racing Association). I will write more about this in the book 'The Greyhound Whisperer. We would to go to trials on a Sunday morning and the old boy Bob working the traps, manually releasing the mechanism so the traps would open. I was only about ten or eleven at the time and our Greyhound Ben, which was his kennel name though he raced under the title 'Mitcham Midget', use to trial and race there a lot and I was always the kennel hand to take charge of the pure muscle running animal. I think old Bob took notice of this and asked my Grandfather if I would give him a hand behind the traps when I wasn't with the dogs. He said yes and I jumped at the chance to be that close to the sport that I had been involved in from such a young age. My first responsibility was to help the owners or handlers put the greyhounds in traps making sure the dog's tail was not caught in the door. I have witnessed part of a tail that had been amputated by the door left in a trap, not nice! Then I was given the job of re-fixing the hare to the metal rod on the inside wire when the race was finished. Finally, Old Bob trusted me enough to let me operate the trap release. There was a white mark painted on the rail which the hare ran on, and as soon as the hare got to that point I had to pull this great big lever in a gap between trap 3 and 4; the traps would fly up and away the dogs went chasing the hare. I did all of this for a fee of two pound a session, which back then wasn't a bad wage for a juvenile. Old Bob saw my Grandfather Tom at various greyhound meetings all over the south east and always asked where I was. The strange thing is, and you really cannot explain it, that not so long ago on 'Talking Pictures' (a channel which shows classic films, TV and long forgotten documentaries) there was a documentary about flapping tracks and would you believe Aldershot, and who did I happen to see appearing in it? Old Bob!

I have never been a person to laze in bed and the only time I frequented my bedroom for any length of time was in 1996 after my nervous breakdown. This was a time for me to heal myself because back then there were no agencies that I could turn to aid in my recovery. In order to get better, and more importantly to stay well, it had to be done through my own determination and inner will. Maybe I got this from my Dad. Around 1980 my he left the Royal Mail because he had enough of working nights constantly. He started working alongside the manager of our youth football team as a skip lorry owner/driver for a well-known waste disposal company based at what is now Old York Road SW18. My Dad would have really early morning starts, sometimes starting between 4am and 6am to get on the road before the London rush hour traffic made driving a hassle. Many a time in my school holidays I would go out with my Dad and ride shotgun. One of the places he used to tip was in a transfer station run by Cappagh plant and skip hire in a yard at the foot of Battersea Bridge right next to the bus garage (now 'The Albion', a block of flats where one apartment has just sold for £6,500,000). As Dad went to work so early, and in the dark, he would tell me to meet him up the chute and pick me up there. I would walk up Battersea Bridge Road to the tip and wait for him. I got talking one day to the owner of the company 'one day' Tommy Cappagh as everybody called him but whose actual name was Tommy Ferncombe and what a great man he was. He asked me once if I would like to help the old Irish boy Phil collect the metal out of the rubbish and he would give me a fiver a day. Now back in 1980 that was a fair wage for a fourteen year old and of course I said yes. I would work from around 7am to about 3pm not only collecting metal but was also taught, by the machine driver Dennis, to drive plant machinery like a Volvo bucket tractor which pushed the rubbish into a neat pile to keep the yard tidy. I also had a go at a Hymac which was the machine with caterpillar tracks and was used to load the tippers to take the rubbish away to a landfill site at Hersham near Walton on the Thames Surrey. On many occasions, if the yard had a quiet period I would go with the tipper driver to tip the load. Hersham Sand and Ballast was an aggregates company that had extracted all the shingle out of massive holes and refilled it with rubbish. This is where, at the tender age of fourteen, I first learned to drive on a DAF 2300 tipper lorry and this was done on the mile and half from the weigh-bridge to the big hole on private land. I had to change gear because of the undulation of the site so this was a great lesson for my driving test which didn't happen for another 3 years. Cappagh Group of companies now has a turnover of £100 million and Tommy is one of the nicest people you could meet. Yes he is a shrewd businessman but foremost a good human being. Tommy looked after his family and many years later when my Mum was a deputy manager in a day centre she cared for Tommy's Mum Bridie. Mum and Dad went to Mrs. Ferncombe's wake. I bumped into Tommy over the years in and around Wimbledon when I was driving lorries and he would always offer me a job driving for him. In many ways, I should have had that experience working with Mr. Cappagh himself. Years later at George's funeral, Dad and I bumped into Tommy again which was a wonderful experience for the pair of us, a bloody good man Tommy Cappagh.

Chapter Fifteen

Notable Brief Encounters

Freddie Mercury and Roald Dahl, who can say they have met these icons of the music and literary worlds? I can (though the good fortune was all a bit of luck). As a youngster I spent an immense amount of time with my Grandfather Tom and Nan Ivy English staying at their 2 bedroom terrace cul de sac home in Morden on the outskirts of London. What you would call the suburbs to me was bliss and the countryside. Grandad was an owner/trainer of greyhounds and had a great deal of success with the sport. When not racing their Dogs it was always a couple of nights out visiting Wimbledon Stadium which then had greyhound racing and also the famous Wimbledon Dons speedway team and Spedeworth International Stock Car Racing Promoters. The stadium has now been demolished. After a week of school I would get home on a Friday and have a bath, say my farewells to Mum and Dad and pack my little brown, with black writing, Adidas sports holdall. Off with a spring in my step for my weekend stay at my Grandparents. I would jump on any bus to Clapham Junction, into the railway station, purchase my ticket (a single to St Helier Station), up onto the platform to catch the first overground train to stop at mainline Wimbledon.

I'd change at to platform 15, which was a loop line service taking me to the station required. I would get on a sort of old-fashioned British Rail train where on shutting the carriage doors you could easily perforate your eardrum! I would arrive at St Helier, a very simple branch line station which Mr. Beeching did not close, where hardly any passengers got off. Straightaway a feeling of peace and tranquility came over me because of I was away from the inner city traffic and noise. Then it was a walk down Glastonbury Road to my Grandparents where my Nan would have waiting for me corned beef and homemade chips made in the most flavoursome lard and 2 buttered slices of bread with a mug of freshly brewed proper tea made with leaves not the imitation tea bags, yuck! To this day I still struggle to have to drink of Britain's favourite beverage made with a teabag. We would set off early for Wimbledon for Friday night racing so 'Fath' as I called him could get a special race card with all the weights, times, split times for the greyhounds racing that night. Nan would get the same seat position she liked in the winning straight glass enclosure. One Friday night outing to Wimbledon, Nan had just got me a burger and chips, Fath his lemonade Shandy and Nan her Whiskey Mac. We sat talking and Fath noticed these four gentleman about three rows below us and said *'that's that singer down there from the Queen, Freddie Mercury'*. My Nan said *'so it is Tommy'*. I have never been a follower of any band, but I had heard of Queen and Freddie Mercury because my exbrother in law was a diehard fan. Strange to say I remembered Queen's 'Bicycle Race' video because some of it contained naked ladies riding around Wimbledon's cinder speedway/stock car track. I had probably seen the daring clip on Top of The Pops. I said *'Julie's boyfriend loves Queen'*, my Grandfather said, *'go and ask him for his autograph for him'*. I said *'no I am a bit shy, he may say no'*, my Grandfather said, *'you have got a 2 to 1 chance of him giving you his autograph which are good odds'*. There was no security with him, no bodyguards in tow so I plucked up the courage to walk about 12 steps of destiny to ask Mr. Mercury. So off I toddled down the steps to ask. He had a couple of other men with him, one I did recognized was the TV and radio comedian Kenny Everett and they were dear friends from when Mr. Mercury appeared on Kenny's Capital Radio show back in 1974 (and no they were never in a relationship just good pals). I said *'Mr. Mercury please may I have your autograph for my sister's boyfriend if it's not too much trouble?'*. He said *'firstly my name is Freddie young man, and it would be my pleasure'*. I was about 14 at the time and I gave him the piece of paper, which was the back of a race card, along with a black bic biro pen. I told him my Sister's boyfriend's name, he wrote *'To Micky, my best wishes Freddie Mercury'*. Although my sister is divorced from him, I still reckon he has the signature to this day (and worth a tidy sum). I wish I had one for myself as an investment. Then again, not many people can say that they were in the presence of, and spoke to, one of the greatest lead singers in the history of rock music.

Another individual I had the serendipitous meeting with was Mr. Roald Dahl. He was probably the greatest children's novelist, poet, screenwriter and wartime fighter with book sales of over 250 million. My Uncle Alan, my Dad' brother, and my Godfather, a self-educated man who was without doubt the most sort after and respected Consulting engineer/motor assessor in the UK, had just purchased his new office space at 3 Turnchapel Mews SW4 (he went on to buy 4 and 5 as well). Turnchapel Mews was a 19th century cobbled courtyard mews. These type of mews were usually located in desirable residential areas of Clapham, having been built to cater for horses, coachmen and stable servants of prosperous residents. The first recorded mews dates back to 1584. Turnchapel Mews must have served the large country house when all around were fields, it was favoured by the wealthier merchant classes of the city of London. Number 3 Turnchapel Mews had a certain character and feeling to it. The stables below the servant's apartments had centuries of work worn cobblestones, with upright wood pillars extending to the ceiling throughout the stables with hollow grooves where the horse had been tethered to the posts. Uncle and I, with my limited expertise, were going to renovate it into workable office space; oh what fun! I use to see this very gaunt gangly gentleman occasionally whilst doing the building work. He was in the habit of saying hello and how are you young man. I was always polite and respectable in my reply and did not think about the gentleman. Uncle never paid me, tight sod, but my treat was to ride my Uncle's secretary Mary's Yamaha 70 up and down the private mews (with crash helmet upon my head for 15 mins before Uncle dropped me home). Again our paths crossed with this gentleman and I wondered if I was annoying him, but once more he was absolutely polite in his communication. He probably just saw a young lad enjoying the experience of going up and down at 10mph and was pretty safe as you could have walked faster than I was riding the motorbike. He knew I was in the safe hands of my Uncle. Then one day my Uncle said to me *'you know who that gentleman you say hello to is?'* I replied *'no I haven't got a clue Uncle, just some old boy'*. Then fireworks went off in my mind when he said *'Its Roald Dahl the Author'*. At junior school I had read 'Charlie and the Chocolate factory' and 'Charlie and the Great Glass Elevator'. I loved the film 'Chitty Chitty Bang Bang' and Mr. Dahl was one of the screenwriters on the intriguing classic British TV series 'The Tales of the Unexpected' (Mr. Dahl also was the creator and based these on his short stories). For years many TV big wigs were trying to get the commissioning rights; its sardonic humorous subdued narrative and the unforeseen about face ending. I adored each episode and the theme tune had a haunting mystical quality to it.

Since the day Uncle told me who that nice old gentleman was, in my encounters from then on it was always '*Mr. Dahl*', '*Good Morning Mr. Dahl*' or '*how are you Mr. Dahl?*' but I never had the courage to tell Mr. Dahl I admired so much his unique and original storytelling style.

At Turnchapel Mews, it is thought Mr. Dahl wrote 'Matilda' and 'Witches'! How lucky was I?

If we only choose to consider sounds and the commotion they stir in our minds, we shall never discover the true principles of music and of its power in our hearts (unknown)

The Genesis for the sound system first became popular in 1940's in Kingston Jamaica. DJ's would load up a truck with a generator, turntables and huge speakers and set up street parties. The culture of the sound system was brought to the UK with the mass migration in the 1950's and 60's. The sound system was the means by which the migrants were able to maintain their cultural connection with the homeland.

'Atlantic Sounds Battersea' was the sound created on the Surrey Lane Estate by a group of my brethren. Massive speakers constructed out of big sheets of six by four MDF and made on the balconies of Frazer and Sancroft Courts. These became the big bass bins, holes the size of manhole covers for the speakers to sit in and little holes at the top for the tweeter to reside; all those double woodwork lessons were worth it. The boys were allowed to set up the sound system on youth club nights at the Surrey Lane Tenants Hall. The bass would shake the windows as they played dubplates. With this the sound system would have a 'toaster' (in other genres called the MC), who would be singing his rhymes and lyrics along to the tunes; all heads nodding. The ginger boy (yours truly) was enchanted by the music as it was like listening to a preacher teaching the gospel. One of the lads is still involved in the sound system scene and is the chairperson of The British Association of Sounds Systems, which includes representing sound systems at the Notting Hill Carnival. He is also a senior manager in the UK Trade and Industry Department and diplomat for the UK government; not bad for a kid from the Surrey Lane?

Chapter Sixteen

A Women for all Seasons and Reasons

My Mum was always there when others were finding life challenging. She stood up against unfairness, abhorred liars and racism made her blood boil. When the Surrey Lane was built, a cheap blow air system was fitted into each property. After a few years, the condensation caused by this system was causing damp in nearly every property and resulted in dark mould patches up the interior walls. The head of Wandsworth Council at the time (who is still a controversial Conservative MP in parliament and likes his voice heard) failed in his leadership by refusing to take landlord responsibility and admit that the blow air system was the problem. When do MP's, governmental figures or departments ever admit that they are wrong? The Surrey Lane Tenants Association meeting was called, and a decision was made to fight the council all the way to court in order that they do their duty as the landlord. My Mum and others from the estate contacted consultants and experts in the field of internal heating systems and they, through examination and experience based on science, created detailed reports proving categorically the blow air systems had caused the damp. These experts were really on our side and charged only a small fee. Off we went to court and the judge ruled in favour of the Surrey Lane and that the council were responsible for the duty and care of the residents; we won the case! As a result, the council had to rip out every blow air system in every single maisonette and tower block and replace it with an internal boiler and up to date radiator system. However, there was never any apology as this may have meant that the local government 'political sheep' were wrong?

On another occasion, my Mum stood up strongly against racism. Our youth football team were playing a Surrey County Youth Cup in a notorious council estate in Surrey that had a mainly white population. It was an ill-tempered match and one of our black players was racially abused by the opposition and was sent off due to his reaction. We went on to win the game with ten men and I don't think our opposition had been beaten for a while. The thought that this was at the hands of a multicultural team from London did not go down too well; we had to vacate this area straight after the match. George, our manager, and my Mum did not believe ethically or morally that this lad had to tolerate racism at any level especially in youth football so challenged the Surrey County FA to a hearing for our teammate in order to rescind his red card. George and my Mum toddled off with a few of us on a cold winter's night to the headquarters of the Surrey FA. Evidence was heard from the match referee and the reasons behind the sending off. George and my Mum got up to speak in favour of our teammate and made a brilliant case. The Surrey FA committee had a conversation between themselves and the red card was rescinded on the evidence of the racial abuse that our teammate had received. Truth won the day and this young lad, my friend and teammate, went on to play for England schoolboys. He also had a career as a professional footballer and represented the first teams at Chelsea, Brentford, Southend United, Charlton Athletic (premier league) and Reading. He also coached at Chelsea Youth Academy, Tooting and Mitcham and then went to America and coached Atlanta Silverbacks Women and Arizona youth club FC Sol. He remains a highly qualified and respected soccer coach in America.

As I have said in earlier tales, mention pie, mash, liquor and stewed or jellied eels to a true Londoner and memories flashback to a time long gone, when pie and mash shops were a plenty. You could get your delicious fine fare in every high street from Tooting to Walthamstow and from the Goldhawk Road to Tower Bridge Road. Sadly, now the majority have vanished with very few shops still in operation. You still can get it delivered online and there are a few that have bucked the trend after the gentrification of London!
Most Saturday evenings Mum and Dad would jump in the car and drive from one side of Battersea to the other to get our grub at Harrington's Wandsworth Road SW8. Again it is long

departed and turned into a Wine bar. The queues where always big outside owing to the limited amount trays of freshly cooked pies that could be baked. If some in front of you had a larger order you had to be patient for the next tray of pies. They even had a miner bird in there who would mimic the staff shouting *'More pies'*. This one faithful day Mum and Dad returned with the food, my cousin was with us for some nosh and the meals were dished out to us all. On getting my grub, I only had two and half pies when I demanded three. I let it be known to my Mum, with constant moaning and gripping, that I was dismayed with the amount I was given and I proceeded to keep on about the fact that I wanted three pies. Being a teenager misbehaviour was part of the 'evolution' (hormones etc.) though pushing the wrong buttons with my Battersea girl Mum....big mistake! My Mum calmly walked into our living room, up to the table I was sitting at with my cousin, and gracefully picked up the plate of sumptuous pie, mash and liquor and said *'do you want this pie and mash'* and tipped it all over my head ! Now there is a moral to this story, don't disrespect your parents even when they put food on the table, and be happy if you get two pies. What's a pie or half a pie when you can have two on your plate! And you've guessed it, ever since that day, with its life lesson, I never once complained about the portion size on my food plate. I was just grateful that I had a meal to eat because thousands go hungry everyday.

On our estate the winter was for football and the summer was for cricket. Along with other sporting activities the Surrey Lane youths enjoyed athletics to tennis to Cricket, etc. We were outside sporty types whatever the weather. At a newsagent we purchased a Wembley football, so light that if the wind caught it the laws of physics did not apply. A wall with a painted wicket was our version of Lords and these were halcyon days.

Most estates in South London staged a yearly event athletics meeting at the Battersea Park running track. The Surrey Lane always entered a team as we had many individuals of natural athletic ability (though not including me). I was attending more as moral support than my turn of speed or prowess. On this one occasion, our four by one hundred relay team were one short and somehow I got coerced into running the third leg which meant I would be running the bend (either my weight giving me greater G in transit or they felt sorry for me!). The three other lads in the team were very athletic and old fat lad was somehow going to aid them in the winning of this relay race. We are all lined up at our hundred metre intervals ready for the race to commence. The race official raises his starting pistol, I had one these guns indoors, BANG, we're off! Our first leg runner on the first bend is up with all the other runners, he passes the baton to the younger brother of our last leg sprinter, his off and it is neck and neck with all the other competitors. As he is coming at me at a turn of speed, I'm off ready to receive the baton, he hands the baton to me, I'm running what seems quick but all the other competitors seem to be running away from me akin to me running in slow motion. By the time I hand over the baton to our last runner we are dead last. Our last runner was in bare feet, and the foundation of Battersea athletics track was black cinder ash, not the modern composition of today. I thought to myself *'oh damn it I have lost the boys the race'*, but what happened next was unbelievable and a feat Usain Bolt would have respected. My relay teammate was off, all I can describe is a big cloud of black cinder ash where his feet were running and it felt that someone had put plus thirty on your sky digital box the speed he was running. I'm shouting at the top of my vocal range with utter bewilderment, not only as he caught up to the others, but ran past them like they were standing still in quick sand. He only won the bloody race! I was shocked and overjoyed, we all embrace in victory and visions in my mind were of the GB team winning Olympic gold. I apologised to my team for the lack lustre speed that I did not possess but really, that did not matter to them, because I took part when no one else would step in. I was completely out of my running comfort zone, and still to this day friends laugh when I point out the one athletics medal in my trophy cabinet.

By this period, around fifteen to sixteen years old, I was in probably the best condition physically I had ever been. In the six-week summer holidays from school I had managed, with total self-discipline and tremendous hard work, to lose a hell of a lot of weight. So much so that when I returned to school in September for the new term my classmates did not recognise me standing in line in the corridor waiting to go into class for our tutor group registration period. I was fed up of being fat and self-conscious of my bulk and boy did I feel better in myself (but not in an egotistical way, more for a better healthy way of life, if you are healthy you are wealthy!).

As a youth football team we were now under the banner connected to Devas Youth Club Stormont Road SW11. We were in a development phase with the quality of our squad of players and stronger opposition every game and not have the mindset that we just needed to turn up in order to win. As a team, right from the conception of our first under eleven squad, we were always immaculately turned out with kits and tracksuits whenever we entered the field of play. It made us feel good, and all out of our leader and manager's pocket. George, our manager, always had faith in me though why I don't really understand. I was not the most technically astute goalkeeper and wasn't ego driven, just the enjoyment and experience with my teammates was enough. I gave my heart and soul in goal and I think unconsciously that is why I lost all the weight. I wanted to discover how good a goalkeeper I could be. I was offered, by my sports teacher at school, a chance to go training at Millwall but I turned it down. We played a cup final at Crystal Palace's training ground and I had a very good game. Their scout asked me if I would be interested in coming youth training. Again I said no because deep down I knew that my dedication and commitment to football was not of a standard to play professionally. I did have a short spell playing non-league at Sutton United and this was after finishing youth football. I even had the chance to play in the FA youth cup, but by then my desire for football was on the wane as my heart was not in it by then. Our first season in the new league saw every game being of a very high standard as we were playing the cream of south London's finest every week. Many of the opposing players were involved with schoolboy training with professional clubs. Our first cup success was the Surrey Invitational Youth Cup. We were under fifteen age playing in the under sixteen age group and we won the trophy at non-league venue Chertsey FC. The final was on a spring Sunday morning and daffodils were everywhere. I can remember plainly having a good performance that kept us in the game. I could dive through the air a lot easier due to not having so much timber surrounding my midriff. I think we went on to win quite comfortably against this team that was an age group above us.

We still had our intense training sessions on Wednesdays and Fridays but now at Sir James Barry School, Patmore Estate (which was my first school and the estate that I was born on). On many occasions we would run from Devas to the training facility, which was about a mile away, and jog back when we had finished the session. I didn't mind because since losing the weight I was quite light on my loafers and most mornings during this period I was up early on school days to do a couple of mile run before I went to school. I was also doing many self-motivating training sessions, with a short trip to Battersea Park, goalie gloves, football boots, ball and myself. I would use the wall by the fountains as a rebound training device by kicking the ball as hard as possible from about ten yards and saving the return. This sharpened my reaction times and made me become comfortable with handling the ball (as my manager drummed into me from a young age ('*Dodger two hands equals catch*'!) and that was a skill I kept all through my goalkeeping career. If I had the chance to catch the ball I always would, only punching and saving when the circumstances needed. In our last year of youth football, which was under sixteens, we truly evolved into a beautifully constructed football team. We played the game as one, we worked hard for five years training two nights a week to become a force in youth football and to have others talk about us with such high esteem. We were never arrogant but committed and determined and took one hundred percent responsibility on the pitch. When you practice a skill long and hard enough it becomes natural and you are then of the mindset ready for improvement; and never complacent. Most of our team at this time were in school boy academies at professional clubs. These included the likes of Arsenal, Chelsea, Fulham, Tottenham and Millwall. The captain of our team (and still a great friend) was at Arsenal at the time but left when he came to the realisation that our beloved football had become just another commercial enterprise (perhaps reflecting the social and economic changes of the early 1980s). That young man went on to be an educator and schoolteacher for over thirty years and recently was put forward for teacher of the year. The majority of my teammates have gone onto become successful businessman and leaders in communities and have had wonderful and varied careers including managing in industry. I believe that this has happened because of the fundamental principles learnt through those football experiences and and life more generally. Leaders without ego are the rarest individuals to find and this can only happen when the desire is for the common good. It is a message for everyone, even when life challenges us, to work hard with integrity, intelligence and to embrace an inner belief that this is the right thing to do. Be generous, be kind and be respectful of others (don't be an arsehole because there are enough in society who do it without any encouragement!).

Our crowning glory, the pinnacle of our youth football years, was winning the under sixteen Surrey Youth Cup which was a top notch and prestigeuous competition. We won the final 5-2 and played the other team off the park. This trophy was not really won on the day but rather the five years previous when we started out as under elevens! This reminds us that success in life is not an overnight achievement, it's a steady progression of goals and learning along the path. Our early life experiences do shape us, the positive and the negative, and are part of the journey to wisdom; and it is wisdom that takes humanity forward. I played football as an adult, but truth be known my heart was never in it after the joy of youth football. I feel blessed to have had George as our manager. He was a great football coach/manager but also an inspiring and motivational leader and a friend to us all. As a soul he was one of life's good guys.

Chapter Seventeen

Free the Hastings Three!

One of my last day trips at school would be remembered for all the wrong reasons and create an infamous legacy. This was a good period in my latter schooling and a rare feeling for me. I was on a CSE motor vehicle course at South Thames College Wandsworth High Street and included a half a day a week escaping from normal lessons, what a touch! I have always had a love for vehicles and the working mechanism of the internal combustion engine so this course was right up my street. I did feel very fortunate to be attending and the course tutor, it turned out, was good friends with my uncle Alan. Both men were highly respected in the UK motor vehicle industry. The Destination for the school trip was Hastings (1066 and all that) and the mode of transport was the train from Clapham Junction. All the fifth year were in attendance and this amounted to about two hundred and forty teenagers all meeting on the platform. The scene made up of us lot made St Tinian's look like Rodean. One of my best friends from school was meant to come but did not turn up which I thought was strange! The testosterone teenage boys arrived in non-uniform clothing which was permitted in the fifth year. The clothing styles included Fila,

Ellesse and Sergio Tacchini tracksuit, maybe a Lyle and Scott or Pringle jumper for visual effect. There were also the Gabicci cardigans with a pair of Farah trousers (the more abstract colour the better) or even a pair of Lois jeans with white ironed seam marks on the front made with a steaming hot iron and damp tea towel by your Mum. There were splits at the bottom to gracefully cover either your Nike Wimbledon, Addias Stan Smith or Diadora Borg Elite Gold. Today these items of clothing are considered casual and retro classics. I had to chuckle a while back as my youngest nephew turned up in an Ellesse garment which I was wearing nye on forty years ago. I thought to myself geezer I must be getting old. I think I attracted female interest back then but I was quite a shy lad when it was time to 'talk the talk' and certainly lacked confidence chatting to girls; I don't think that Blue Stratos or Brutt aftershave scent was a natural aphrodisiac anyway!

All the unruly pupils boarded the train with teachers shouting at the top of their voices to keep us in order then patrolling up and down the corridors of the train carriages just in case one of us decided it would be fun to pull the emergency red brake cord to get the train stopped instantly. However, we made it to Hastings without drama and were told, non-negotiably, to meet back at the station at a certain time for our transit back to old London Town. I paired up with two mates, one off my estate and one off the estate across the road from the Surrey Lane for our never to forget experience in the historical town of Hastings. We were not there for a history fact finding of the Norman conquest, or King Offa with his tribes invading Sussex and Kent. No we were there as a marauding tribe from a place in south London, led by the elders. These were made up of a couple of Maths teachers with ill-fitting clothes and suede shoes, a couple of English teachers who started teaching when inkwells were still in desks and a science teacher who had a nervous tic movement with his neck which gave him the lovely impression of a chicken! Finally, we had a couple of History and Social Studies teachers who were only there for the history and if there was a revolution on the route they were in. Half anti-establishment and half establishment they had a conflict of conscience. With jeans and a crisp white shirt with a tie they only partly fulfilled the teacher's dress code. They were stereotypical university activists and I would imagine they'd be up the front of the protests with their Che Cuevara T shirts, placards in hand whilst puffing a king size reefer (as they always looked stoned to me). Hasting only had a few entertainment spots like the East Cliff funicular railway, which once you had been up and down the enjoyment was over. There was a boating lake and a few basic fairground rides. The fishing trawlers were launched at day break from the stoney, pebble laden beach by tractor and winch and when they returned from their fish catching expedition the mechanics of departure were repeated but in reverse in order to lay their vessels lopsided on the beach like stranded pilot whales. We three were bored by now. We had done most of our money and so wondered where our other mate was (the one who didn't turn up on the day). So we thought we would give him a ring. Both the boys I was with were in his tutor group so both knew him quite well. We found a telephone box, the K6 (kiosk number 6) public telephone designed by Sir Giles Scott, which nowadays goes for good money. This is a British cultural icon and was voted in Britain's top ten designs ever along with the likes of the Mini, the Routemaster bus and the Spitfire. But alas, we were not in the telephone box for its aesthetics as they usually stank of piss with graffiti on the inside with quotes like 'Jesus saves, but Keegan gets the rebound'. No, we were only going to enter the box so we could find out where our mate was who let us down.

So the lad off the estate opposite, who did not weigh two stone soaking wet, and I entered the phone box to ring our missing mate, whilst the other boy who was a bit of a big lad waited outside because all three of us could not fit into the small space.

I rang his number, two pence perched on the entrance to the coin opening and with anticipation for the pips to sound and that was the time to push my money into the slot. But all it kept doing was ringing without any answer, the skinny mate and I decided then to give up, but our mate outside decided it would be a laugh to hold the door fast so we could not get out. At this time I was not the rotund proportion of my former slef, so both of us could not budge the telephone box door for love nor money. I decided to spin myself round and wedge my feet up against the opposite side with back to the door in a scissor like jack configuration. The intention was to prize the door open but at this time, with my 28 inch waist and my arse being quite skinny, the force of my exertion pushed my bottom out if one of the small rectangle glass panels, smashing it and falling onto the floor. Unbeknown to us right opposite were the local East Sussex Constabulary, parked up in a Mk2 Escort Panda watching the exploits of these inner city kids. The copper got out of the car and bellowed, *'you three stay where you are. I want to have a word with you'*. We did think about running but the bulky lad could not run, neither could he walk very far due to his flat feet. The Officer came over to us and we thought he'd to give us a reprimand but instead said, *'you three are nicked for criminal damage'*. I tried to explain it was a total accident and how we were on a school trip from London and I don't think that helped the situation and all three of us were bundled into police vehicles and we were on our way to Hastings police station. We had only been in the town for two and a half hours!

We arrived at the cop shop and were swiftly marched into the custody area, *'Criminal damage'* the PC said to the desk sergeant. I tried to explain what had happened but again to no avail. All three of us were put into a holding room (because of our age the law stated we were not to put into the cells) thank heavens. My fat lad mate still had his packed lunch of liversausge sandwiches with HP sauce and was more concerned whether the coppers were going to confiscate them! I was starting to realise the gravity of the situation and wanted one of the police officers to come back in so that we could plead with him to let us go. We were in this room for ages so had loads of time to come up with all different explanations for the damage to the telephone box. My mind was racing with images of good cop, bad cop and whether are they were going to beat the truth out of us for accidentally breaking a telephone box window? It did seem like a lifetime in the room but was probably only about four hours. Then we heard the key turning in the locked door, the policeman came in and behind him was one of our teachers with a face like thunder. He did not look a happy bunny, *'What the bloody hell were you three clowns doing?'*. I replied by trying to explain what happened and why. One of the other pupils on the trip had seen us get nicked and only notified the teacher when everyone had met at the station to catch the train back to good old London Town. *'Come with me and don't say a word '* he said. The officer who arrested us kindly gave us a lift back to the train station for us to be greeted by all the pupils cheering and laughing at our foolish exploits. We were made to sit right by the teachers all the way back, with the quietness of a leaf falling to ground upon the onset of autumn.

The teachers had already told me to report to the headmaster's office first thing when I got into school the next day. I was on my journey back home upon the top deck of a number 19 Routemaster bus encased in as much fog as a native american Indian sending smoke signals. In those days you could smoke upstairs but that wasn't my concern at the time but rather what the hell was my Mum going to say; or do I even tell her? Up to our front door I trudged, shoulders dropped like I was due for the guillotine and the loss of my head. Dad answers the door and I go into our front room and Mum asks, *'had an enjoyable day Butch?'*. My reply was muted, *'well Mum, you could call it enjoyable or you could call it a bit different to other school trips'*. My Mum could read me like a book and it felt like she was sensing what I was feeling and thinking both.

'What happened?'

'Well, I got arrested'.

'How the hell did you get arrested on a day trip?

My Dad was there but just sitting quietly while Mum cross-examined me.

'Criminal damage, criminal damage to what? A telephone box! Did you smash it up?'

'No I put my arse through a window and sitting right opposite was a copper, two others got arrested as well'.

'I'm not worried about the others, did you get charged?'

'No we got off with a caution and a year ban from Hastings'.

Mum just shook her head and gave me a few choice words in a certain expression and language not appropriate for this story. The bollocking was over and the Battersea girl got her message across and as my parents always made sure that it was always about learning the lesson; just guiding us gently back onto the truthful path.

I woke up the next morning to get ready for school with anxieties about what the Headmaster was going to say. Off on my twenty minute walk to school, not to my tutor group but straight up to the Headmaster's office. I had a very good relationship with him as he had taught me RE for for three years and this included the last year of secondary school; but was this all about to change?

I stood outside the office which was on a long corridor overlooking the courtyard of the school. The deputy head walked past, he used to teach me physics, *'what have we been up to Mr. English?'* he said. I replied *'I got arrested Sir'*. With a shake of his head he retorted, *'well that was a day with a difference my boy'*, and went into his office which was next door to the Headmaster. I am standing thinking to myself what have I done? I have nearly completed my CSE college motor vehicle course and was in the process of filling out an application form for a City and Guild Motor Vehicle technology part 1 and 2. This was my chance for a route into gainful employment as a trainee bus mechanic. I could have easily balls it all up. Then I heard this big booming voice, *'Stephen would you like to come into my office please'*. My Headmaster was always military smart, shoes with a reflection you could use as a mirror, a suit so well maintained it felt like it had just come out of John Colliers window. He had the tone of voice that made you realise that when he spoke you listened (it was comparable to a drill sargent). *'Sit yourself down Stephen'* he said, *'I've heard others perspective now let me hear yours because I know you will tell the truth'*. I told him the story of why we were in the phone box and my concern for my mate and how it was a total accident. I mentioned us being foolish and how it felt bad that I had brought shame on the school.

'Have you still got your Good News Bible?' was his response (these were given to us by him in the first year when we started RE).

'Yes I have Sir'.

'Some people ruin themselves by their own stupid actions and then blame others. You didn't, You accept what you have done and have taken the blame upon your own shoulders'.

'Yes Sir' I said. who knows where he was going with this.

'People who listen when they are corrected will live a fulfilling life Stephen. If you are good you will be guided by honesty'.

'Yes Sir' I said though he has lost me now.

'You didn't hide the truth, you told me the truth because I knew I could trust you'. 'If you say so Sir'.

'Teach a child how to live and he will remember all his life (Proverbs 22:6)'.

'I hope so Sir'.

'Stephen, when I mentioned that you would benefit from RE in the Fourth and Fifth year, I bet you scorned the idea'. Does Sir want me to be a Vicar? I'm sitting there totally taken in by what he is saying but not really understanding just like in the presence of a sage.

'Stephen you have great ethics and a deep principle of life, a goodness'.

'Have I Sir?'

As I now reflect, the realisation dawns that life will throw us many challenges but it is how we learn from these experiences that make us the better person. So, it was nn your way Stephen, lesson over, and that was it. There was no being shouted at, no suspension, no exclusion, no detention and it's taken me years to work out that my old Headmaster educated me in proverbs. This was the best talk from any teacher in all of my school days because it sunk in. It influenced my consciousness and made me realise that the meaning of life is to discover your gift and that the purpose of life is to give it away.

Chapter Eighteen

The Past and The Present - What were the Lessons?

What did I learn about from first sixteen years of life growing up in a working class environment on a council estate? Well that everyone is equal no matter their financial status. On our estate the highest level of a skilled worker was represented by my mate's dad who was a beautiful man but sadly no longer with us. He was a furniture upholsterer and his son followed in his trade. There was poverty on the Surrey Lane with families on extremely low incomes but never once was there judgement. Many times residents on the estate had to knock on our door asking to borrow a fiver as otherwise their children would go hungry. My Mum was always willing to help others without question. As a family we were not flush with money but helping others was always part of our family principles. Giving from the heart and not getting lost in the blind alley of logic. I know that my Mum grew up in a low income family so always had empathy when others were struggling.

When you grow up from a tender age in a multicultural community you learn that we were all brothers and sisters, all connected, we were all one. Even now when I visit Battersea (which isn't often), where my character and personality started to evolve, old friends off the Surrey Lane still talk about my parents with great affection and utmost respect. My Mum and Dad were always greeted as Mr English or Miss English (although my Mum was married!). On reflection with my Mum's passing the outpouring of grief totally surprised me. Lifelong friends from Surrey Lane and Battersea told how important a figure my Mum was and how she and my Dad played such impoirtant roles in their lives. My Mum played a role of second, surrogate mother in many young lives and our family unit was admired for the pure unconditional love which was always there and shared in abundance. My Sister and I still have conversations about this topic and to us it was just normal but we realise that to many it was not. With single parents, poverty and fractured family relationships being common all around us, you did not know what went on behind closed doors. This is why modern society frustrates me with its selfishness, narcissistic mindsets and a 'me, me, me' attitude where the individual has little care for others. If all meaning in life is based on external materialistic wealth I'm afraid you will never be truly happy and content. We have to return to caring for each other as we did on the Surrey Lane and Battersea; a heart to heart connection instead of the haves and the have nots, pull the ladder up Jack, I'm OK, I'm not concerned with you! Caring, compassion, gratitude and kindness will move humanity to a better state of balance. A smile is a universal language, an 'hello' to a stranger maybe the only person that individual has spoken to that day. Please just be nice to everyone it does not hurt. True principles and values go a long way; and love even further!

Though I may have not fitted into the structure of standardised education it never defined me. In fact it unconsciously made me more determined to achieve because I have had employment and careers others only dream of. I sort of came to a realisation in my last year of schooling that I and I alone was the master of my life. Looking back it is sad that our schooling was characterised by voices that were always dismissive, in other words *'shut up and do your work or get out of the class'*.

I hope that we have moved on and that eductaors are more inclined to help our young people evolve in character and personality in order to reach their full potential in this thing called life.

It has taken me 54 years to work out what my life purpose is. It has meant battling the system of conformity, going against everything told to do by peers who have never lived the life I have and shall never understand because they have never experienced the circumstances. I believe schooling (and I may have had said it before!) should not teach you what to think but how to think. Wherever you are reading this, there are far too many lost souls having been taken far too soon because life lacked meaning or it got too challenging. I have had very close friends take their own life. I had one who had tried prior to my speaking with him after recovering from the nervous breakdown. We were chatting at a friend's house and he just came out with it, totally innocently, in a conversation, *'Dodger I tried to kill myself'*. I was stunned. My friend was the last person I ever thought would try to attempt such a thing. I asked him why and he said *'because life's crap, too hard and it's not worth the aggro. But it's lovely seeing you get better Dodger'*. Two weeks later he was dead! I read an article recently about a young man whose exams were cancelled and so he took his own life because he didn't want to end up in a dead end job. That dead end job statistic was ME from my state education! Another young man of 16 from a single parent family who was from the estate was well known to the feds (police) and a younger, then elder, in a notorious local gang. I knew his Uncle very well as we were the same age. I asked him one day why he did what he did and how he saw his future. This is what he said,

'Dodger man, I ain't got a future. My Dad left us because he couldn't handle responsibility. He was my hero but now he's inside. He's never given my Mum anything. He never even told me he loved me. My Mum works all hours for two hundred notes. I can earn that in a day selling my weed. I feel like my bruvs (gang) are my family and love. I got slung out of school at thirteen because I got caught with a zoot in the playground. School can't control me, the feds are pussies and racist. Eight times I got a tug last week but I put my gear in the bin rooms and only get what I need so was clean when the pigs search me. All I know is the Lane. Uncle tells me about the past on the Lane and Battersea so wish I was born in them times. It's scary out there Dodger man for the youth them. You never know if it will be your last day living. No qualifications, no prospects, no hope.

I have no value in my life, is this it? Selling gear for the rest of my days?'

I lost contact with him when I moved out of London but heard from a friend of a friend that he is now doing ten years for robbing post offices and newsagents. What a waste of a young life.

This brings us to the inevitable question of where responsibility lies. As these chronicles make clear there was so much to commend about the care that our community had for those that were struggling, in whatever form that took. However, the last forty years have seen massive social changes that have had very detrimental unwanted consequences. For instance, the closure of youth clubs, redundancy of youth workers and general funding cuts.

Are schools preparing our younger generations for the realities of life? Do they discuss the pain, the suffering, the hurt, the loss, the experience of lessons that life will teach them? No, I don't believe so. The concern is about exam grades instead of mental health, wellbeing and a deeper understanding of life skills to prepare for the 'head mess' that life is at times. As a youngster growing up I had never heard of the term 'anxiety'(I couldn't even spell it!) and the term depression was not a word as freely used as it is today. Only recently, our paperboy's friend, a thirteen year old, had a year off school suffering from anxiety. What are we doing to these young minds or perhaps the question should be what are we not doing for them? Are we putting labels on too many people, whether young or old? A friend of mine who was a youth leader said to keep the youth club open he had to apply for funding and grants every sixteen weeks. There is a saying by William Wordsworth which summarises how we might move forward wisely,

'Life is divided into three terms - that which was, which is, and which will be. Let us learn from the past to profit by the present, and from the present, to live better in the future'.

My last stage of school was probably the most enjoyable because I knew I was leaving. I had a new form teacher who I really connected with; he just got me, didn't try to change me and accepted me. He was the only teacher who treated me as an equal (rather than the dictatorial figures who never listened). We became good friends as I went on to play for his old boys grammar school cricket team that he had played in for many years. I carried on playing for a long time after my school days had finished. In my final year I was invited to play for the teachers cricket team. I think they passed me off as a student teacher and it was a very strange paradox that I was calling them 'Sir' at school but by their first names at the games of football and cricket.

Exams were just on the horizon and we were given six weeks study leave to revise, which meant for me doing nothing. I spent most of my time over Battersea Park and out enjoying myself because I could not wait to leave school if truth be told. My exams were taken, five years state education in a forty five minute multiple choice test, and you can guess that my grades were rubbish; E's and unclassifieds and a DNTU (did not turn up). Would you believe it that, at the end of school presentation, I did get a prize book token for sport; who knows how the hell I achieved that! Long before the end of my schooling I had the foresight to apply for employment. I only sent off two application forms, one for Jack Barclays (a Roll Royce dealer as an apprentice motor mechanic but I did not have the right exams grades) and the other to London Transport as a bus mechanic garage trainee. The latter was a lesser version of an apprenticeship but still involved Motor Vehicle Technology City and Guilds part 1 and 2 at Paddington Green College one day a week. I was successful in this and was invited for an interview and another test. I kept it quiet from my teachers and even our school careers officer. He gave us no hope of having a meaningful working career and just saw us as more school leavers filling manual employment; because that was what state schools were all about, right!

Chapter Nineteen

Battersea

Battersea is a great symbol of what has gone awry with community spirit and society in general. In the early eighties Battersea was given the title South Chelsea because of the influx of yuppies that started to invade and gentrify the area. There has always been well to do residents in Battersea ('Posh' we would call them). However, there was a mutual respect and a knowing that we did not mix in each other's social circles. The new influx, which started in the 1980's, were totally different. A friend who happens to be a Count (and no I have not put an 'o' in by accident!) told me why this was so. He said *'Dodger these little rich kids who have never wanted for anything, are given untold wealth by their parents. Let us say mummy and daddy gave them 10 million pound. Instead of them paying for a house in say Lyall Mews SW3 at 7 million and only have 3 million to play with, they are paying five hundred thousand for the same place in say Kelmscott Mews SW11 and saving nine and half million. For this they can drink the finest wines and champagne and throw cocaine up their nose and never do a proper days work in their lives'.* However, I need to share a different and altogether wonderful tale about a lady who moved in next door. Her name was Ursula and this was the middle of the 1980's and she lived there until she passed away recently. Now this lady was posh, when I mean posh to a Battersea person that is someone who pronounces all their vowels in a conversation. She was a single middle aged lady who had been to the best private schools and her father was a canon. She was academically well educated and had a career at a bespoke South American travel agent serving the ultra-rich. She could have lived anywhere and It puzzled me why this lady from a different class and culture would choose to live on the Surrey Lane? One day I plucked up the courage to ask her *'why the bloody hell did you choose to live here as you do?'*. She replied, *'well Stephen, lots of people with lots of money are not very nice people, the majority tend to look down on the less educated and not so fortunate, they are very pretentious (I had to look that word up back then because I did not understand what it meant). I deal with these individuals every day and they are somewhat boring and tiresome. I was very nervous moving on to the Surrey Lane from my background but not one person on this block or estate has judged me. You have all accepted me. I feel a sense of love that I have never experienced before in my life and back when I first moved in when you did not even know me you said "you alright love, how you settling in? If you ever need anything just give us a knock, anyone on this balcony their doors are always open". That made me feel a part of a real community with spirit, a realness to life which I have never had before. Your Mother Eileen and your Father John are such kind and caring people. You are educating me about what's important in life'.* That was our beautiful posh neighbour who we thought the world of.

Battersea, sadly, has been comprehensively gentrified and along with social engineering has depleted the community, character, spirit and soul which was the essence of Battersea. Those whom I call true Battersea people can no longer afford to live there and the upmarket cafes and bars are the outward sign of this (back in my day if we saw tables and furniture outside that was called eviction!). I am sorry to say that money and superficiality has dismantled Battersea. This does hurt me as someone who has had family and heritage in the area dating back to 1538, though I know and understand that I can't stop the progress of materialism based on greed.

However, I will hold in my heart and soul the Battersea motto wherever life shall take me:

NOT FOR YOU, NOT FOR ME, BUT FOR US!

Printed in Great Britain
by Amazon